W9-AQT-646

TWAYNE'S WORLD AUTHORS SERIES

A Survey of the World's Literature

Sylvia E. Bowman, Indiana University

GENERAL EDITOR

FRANCE

Maxwell A. Smith, Guerry Professor of French, Emeritus
The University of Chattanooga
Visiting Professor in Modern Languages
The Florida State University

EDITOR

Montesquieu

(*TWAS 38*)

TWAYNE'S WORLD AUTHORS SERIES (TWAS)

The purpose of TWAS is to survey the major writers —novelists, dramatists, historians, poets, philosophers, and critics—of the nations of the world. Among the national literatures covered are those of Australia, Canada, China, Eastern Europe, France, Germany, Greece, India, Italy, Japan, Latin America, New Zealand, Poland, Russia, Scandinavia, Spain, and the African nations, as well as Hebrew, Yiddish, and Latin Classical literatures. This survey is complemented by Twayne's United States Authors Series and English Authors Series.

The intent of each volume in these series is to present a critical-analytical study of the works of the writer; to include biographical and historical material that may be necessary for understanding, appreciation, and critical appraisal of the writer; and to present all material in clear, concise English—but not to vitiate the scholarly content of the work by doing so.

Montesquieu

By J. ROBERT LOY
City University of New York

Twayne Publishers, Inc. :: New York

Library of Congress Catalog Card Number: 67–25200

MANUFACTURED IN THE UNITED STATES OF AMERICA

To The Memory Of
FRANK A. RUSSO

Teacher and Humanist
Colleague and Friend
1906–1964

Preface

This short study does not claim to add significantly to Montesquieu scholarship; it was not written for scholars. On the other hand, it has not been concocted as a painless rehash of what every college student should know about Montesquieu. It will best serve its purpose if read along with the important texts of the author studied—preferably read after *The Persian Letters* and *The Spirit of Laws.*

The reader is not expected to love or even to like Montesquieu. But it is hoped that he will find himself involved with the problems that Montesquieu set himself. They are problems of men living in society and since man, by definition, lives in society, they are perennial. A bit of reflection will permit the serious reader of Montesquieu to gauge just how far his contemporary society has come in solving them. He will then form his own estimate of Montesquieu's contribution to humanity—not because older heads have called *The Spirit of Laws* an important book, not because the name Montesquieu appears on reading lists of the obvious, but because the reader has hopefully come to know the man and his works with some understanding and with good will if not sympathy.

The best place to start, of course, is with *The Persian Letters* entire, followed by at least substantial portions of *The Spirit of Laws.* A little laughter followed by a little personal thought never hurt anyone, as both Rabelais and Montesquieu would agree.

J. ROBERT LOY

City University of New York
Brooklyn, N. Y.

Contents

MONTESQUIEU

by

J. ROBERT LOY

This study is a life-and-works of Montesquieu, treating first the life, then the works, both descriptively and thematically, his role in Western thought and his contribution to literature and the social sciences. It is intended as a general introduction for students of various disciplines at the college undergraduate level—an introduction to the eighteenth century in France as well as to the works of Montesquieu. Equal attention has been given to literary considerations and central ideas; thus, the book is useful to students of comparative literature as well as the social sciences.

It presupposes a concurrent reading of at least some texts of Montesquieu's writings, particularly THE PERSIAN LETTERS and THE SPIRIT OF LAWS. Although rough outlines of these and other works have been provided, the greater insistence is placed upon an analysis of thematic problems to which Montesquieu's works give rise.

Chronology

1685 Revocation of The Edict of Nantes. France suffers loss of Protestant population active in commerce.
1688 James II deposed in England; William and Mary on throne after Glorious Revolution.
1689 Bill of Rights passed in British parliament in January. January 18, Charles-Louis de Secondat (Montesquieu) born at Chateau de la Brède.
1694 François-Marie Arouet (Voltaire) born in Paris.
1696 Montesquieu's mother dies.
1700–1705 Montesquieu in private church school (Oratorians) outside Paris at Juilly.
1705–1708 Montesquieu studies law at Bordeaux. August, 1708, receives law degree and accepted as "avocat" in Bordeaux parlement. (He takes his uncle's name: becomes Charles-Louis de Secondat de Montesquieu, Seigneur Baron de la Brède.)
1709–1713 Continues practice of law in Paris.
1711 Composes an essay (now lost) "On the Eternal Damnation of Pagans," showing that philosophers of antiquity do not deserve damnation.
1712 Birth of J.-J. Rousseau.
1713 Montesquieu's father dies. The papal bull *Unigenitus* condemns 101 propositions of Quesnel's *Moral Reflexions*. Victory for the Jesuits; Jansenists go underground. Birth of Denis Diderot.
1714 Accepted as "conseiller" in Bordeaux parlement.
1715 Marries Jeanne de Lartigue, of good local family and an ardent Protestant. Death of Louis XIV.
1716 His uncle dies. He inherits the uncle's title (henceforth he is Baron de Montesquieu) and his position, *président à*

mortier in Bordeaux parlement, and all his property. He is accepted as member of Academy of Sciences at Bordeaux. He writes two essays: "Roman Policy in Religion," and "System of Ideas."

1716–1720 The financial "system" of John Law under the Regency of Duke of Orleans (for child King Louis XV).

1718 Two essays read before Academy: "Discourse on the Cause of Echo," "Discourse on the Role of the Kidneys."

1719 Pages on a project for *Physical History of the Earth, Both Ancient and Modern.*

1720 "Discourse on Cause of Weight in Bodies." "Discourse on Cause of Transparency in Bodies."

1721 "Observations on Natural History." *The Persian Letters* published.

1723 The regent Duke of Orleans dies.

1722–1725 Years in Paris. Social and intellectual life: milieu of Duke of Bourbon (new regent for Louis XV), *salon* of Mme de Lambert and others, Entresol Club where he reads "Dialogue of Sylla and Eucrates."

1725 *The Temple of Cnidus,* Montesquieu's exercise in *galanterie.*

1726 Fleury replaces Bourbon as first minister to Louis XV, now king in own right. Montesquieu sells his position as *président à mortier* at Bordeaux.

1728 Montesquieu elected to French Academy, thanks in part to feminine politics and overlooking on part of officialdom of his *Persian Letters.*

1728–1731 Travels in Europe (Austria, Italy, Germany, Holland) and in England.

1731 Voltaire's *Philosophic* (*or English*) *Letters;* Prevost's *Manon Lescaut.*

1731–1748 At La Brède, working on his *magnum opus.*

1734 Publication of *Considerations on the Causes of the Grandeur and Decadence of the Romans.*

1748 Publication of *The Spirit of Laws.*

1749 Attacks from all sides: Jansenist, Jesuit and *philosophe.* Diderot's *Letter on the Blind.*

1750 Montesquieu publishes *Defense of the Spirit of Laws.* Rousseau's *First Discourse.*

1751 Despite Montesquieu's well-meant efforts, *Spirit of Laws* put on Index by Rome. First volume of *Encyclopédie*.
1754 Montesquieu writes "Essay on Taste" for the *Encyclopédie*.
1755 Montesquieu dies, February 10, at Paris. Earthquake in Lisbon.

CHAPTER 1

The Man

Je vais commencer par une sotte chose qui est ma généalogie.[1]

I *Family*

FOR the reader eager to get on to essentials, nothing so boring as an interminable examination of old records (yellowing birth certificates and property deeds); to the interested disciple, nothing so fascinating as these same documents written in an impossible legal hand. Since Montesquieu himself (in his *Pensées*) found justification for starting with such a stupid thing as his family background, we need no other. For he saw, as we shall see, that his particular frame of mind, the "spirit" of the man, owed something to his roots.

The fourth generation of Secondats preceding the writer takes us back in time to the evil days of religious wars in France and to Jean de Secondat, son of Pierre de Secondat, faithful liege of Jeanne d'Albret and partisan now of the Catholics, now of the Protestants. His second son, Jacob de Secondat, saw long military service in the Low Countries, was gentleman of the chamber to the good King Henri IV and received from him the title of baron, for the lands of Montesquieu had been elevated to a barony. Originally a Protestant, he, like his lord, the king, converted to Catholicism. His son Gaston de Secondat was *président à mortier*[2] of the Guyenne parlement, a Catholic, and father of six sons, to the eldest of whom he would grant the office of *président à mortier.* The other five sons were all to enter the Church with reasonable hopes for clerical preference from Gaston's friend, the famous minister Colbert. The third son, however, chose military service and after a distinguished career, married in 1686 a certain Marie-Françoise de Pesnel whose dowry brought into the family the baronetcy and château of La Brède, southeast of Bordeaux. Their first son and our writer, Charles-Louis de Secondat was born February 18, 1689, at La Brède. His mother was to die seven years later. His father died the year of the controversial Constitution or *Unigenitus* bull in 1713. The father's elder brother, he who had received the office of *président à mortier,* will die three years later. Upon Charles-Louis will fall then the titles of Baron de la Brède (from his mother), the property of the Secondats through his father and the *présidence à mortier,* as well as the additional title, Baron de Montesquieu, from his uncle. It is this latter name that Charles-Louis de Secondat, Baron de la Brède et de Montesquieu, will make famous as author of the *Spirit of Laws.*[3]

For at least two reasons, the family background is important. The Secondat-Montesquieu family, *noblesse de robe,* was neither obscure nor arriviste; it had significant roots in a vital moment of modern French history and comfortable roots in the social life of Gascony. Montesquieu will never feel apologetic about his title; on the contrary, it is a source of quiet contentment. The religious evolution of the family during the difficult times of religious upheaval had, no doubt, its own particular significance for Montesquieu. In 1715 (year of the death of the aged Sun King), he had made a good marriage to Jeanne de Lartigue. She was then, and continued to be with unquestioned resolve, a Protestant. In a nation where, after the revocation of The Edict of Nantes,[4] it was not always easy to be a Protestant, Montesquieu must often have considered the personal belief of his wife before assuming public attitudes and reconciling private interests. Indeed one might say that his early interest in religious criticism (an interest that continued until his death) was the necessary predisposition for his larger critical sounding of the laws. That internal dialogue stretching over a lifetime might have been quite different in a man without Montesquieu's comfortable pride in his title, without his long-standing involvement in the minority religion.

II *Self-Portrait*

Je vais faire une assez sotte chose: c'est mon portrait.[5]

However stupid we are to judge the attempt to essay one's own character sketch, we must be alertly grateful for Montesquieu's self-limned portrait as entrusted to his *Pensées*. I think we are struck first of all here by the healthiness of the person. Montesquieu does not tire of telling us how sound his physical constitution is (he calls it his *machine*), how happy have been his relationships with the ladies, how contented he is with his lot and his role as baron de Montesquieu. For the student of post-Romantic literature, there seems something almost indecent in Montesquieu's confession that he "wakes up every morning with a secret joy; I see the daylight with a kind of delight. All the rest of the day, I am content." [6] No tensions, no Freudian erosions, no feelings of inadequacy or gnawing ambition. Who is this man, so complacent, to have nonetheless spent his lifetime writing a book to challenge the very contentment he so loves? The explanation is perhaps too simple, but it goes far toward explaining the man. "My soul," says Montesquieu, "seizes upon everything." [7] And soul is clearly the word he meant to use, not here a Cartesian substitute for mind. For Montesquieu's soul is his machine *and* his mind *and* his emotions (as he calls them, in good eighteenth-century style, my sentiments or my heart). Everything that is alive justifies being alive. Everything may not be *right* (*pace* Pope and Leibnitz), but everything is worthy of observation and classification or, at least, an attempt at classification. One must suppose that he did not arrive at such a quiet philosophy at once; indeed there is continuing evidence in his personal thoughts and written works to show that two intellectual and emotional points of view are always in play. The baron de Montesquieu ought to know that the French monarchy (echoing Bossuet's apologies for it) is the optimum system of order for a baron and a Catholic. But there are other voices (Protestant, for example) and other rooms (England and Persia, for example) that make such comfortable absolutes untenable. At such moments, there enters Montesquieu, the citizen of the world—by actual travel or armchair travel in books. And then everything that is, is interesting because it is and not because it is good or best. This conviction of relativity that is the center of *The Persian Letters* and the formative genius of the *Laws*, is also and in prior fashion the explanation of the man.

Although satisfied with his lot and, as a good Frenchman, happy in society—the society of the great and near-great gathered together inevitably under the charm or strong personality of a woman—Montesquieu was scarcely a social lion. Indeed, like Rousseau later, he was timid in society and many are the stories of disappointment told by those who expected the famous *président* to be brilliant and witty. He suffered, as so many first-rate minds have, from what the French call stair-case wit: i.e., he thought of what he might have said only as he was leaving. What, perhaps naturally, he most disliked were those who did know how to sparkle in company, proffering witticisms with little substance—the very stuff of social success. "When people expected me to be brilliant in conversation, I never was. I preferred having a man of parts to uphold me rather than ninnies to approve of me." [8] This does not prevent him, all the same, from recounting the occasional *bons mots* he found for the occasion as he visited the crowned heads and the great of Europe. But one must believe him honest when he disclaims interest in court intrigue—a sure way to arrive, at least temporarily. Very probably, he had seen too much of the scandals of the Orleans Regency, the excesses of Mr. Law's financial system, and the feeble efforts of Orleans' successor, the Duke of Bourbon, to be impressed by that crowd. There is a whole sentimental education in the following reflections taken from his *Pensées* on his own character: "Upon first seeing most of the great, I was seized with juvenile fear. So soon as I got to know them, I passed, almost without transition, to scorn." "I hate Versailles, because everyone there is little. I like Paris because everyone there is great." "I should rather drive in my coach with a whore than with the Count of Ch——; because I should prefer people to think I had a vice rather than bad taste." [9] No, society with all its pettiness was fine and the Court diverting, but this was not the end of living: "I never tried to make my fortune by way of the Court; I thought rather to make it by developing my property and thus have my fortune directly from the hand of the gods." [10] Paris was necessary (and who could want to live without it?), but home was otherwise attractive: "Whilst I was in the world of society, I loved it as if I could not possibly stand to leave it. When I was on my own lands, I thought no more of society." [11]

He speaks singularly little of his wife, who had brought him a good dowry, a good name, and a good head (if not great beauty), and who was an excellent mother and housekeeper, caring for their estates through law suit and financial pinch while the lord of the manor was in Austria, England, or Paris. And perhaps, for the good eighteenth-century husband, such a blessed state of domestic efficiency made it unnecessary to speak of one's wife.[12] In *The Persian Letters* he suggests that she had a strange quirk of limping but only if she knew she was being watched. In general, one must suppose that the marriage was neither better nor worse than most eighteenth-century domestic arrangements; there was, happily, precious little insistence on that kind of togetherness which later ages have assumed to guarantee a happy match. Of his children he says not much, although it is clear that he was very close to them and in particular to his daughter, who served him for a while as a sort of secretary. All is probably said on this score when he notes (in the *Pensées*): "With my children, I lived as with my friends." [13]

His office as *président à mortier* he took as seriously as he thought the position merited; his thoughts thereon might surprise some of his readers. At the time he inherited the office from his uncle he lacked by significant years the age of forty required for such office. It took him from 1716 until 1723 to obtain the requisite dispensation—meanwhile, in good Regency fashion, occupying his office. Thirty-four in that year, he waited only two more years to sell the *présidence* at an attractive price. One must suppose that financial solvency and his own secret intellectual pursuits were at that time more important than the challenge or honor of the *présidence*.[14] Other considerations might have entered into his decision: his desire to live frequently in Paris, his eye turned toward the French Academy, and the heightened general animosity in France toward Protestants when a Protestant was keeper of his home. What he has to say about his post in the *Pensées* is informative, however curt: "As to my job of *président*, I was quite honest about it; I understood well enough the questions themselves; but, as to the procedure, I understood not a whit. And yet I had applied myself seriously. But what discouraged me most was that I could discern in stupid oafs this same talent that, so to speak, escaped me." [15] One might conclude that the man capable of spending his life in search of the spirit of law could find little interest in and courage for the pedestrian, every-day application of existing laws.

All in all, by his own witnessing, Montesquieu might strike the reader as a singularly reasonable—that is to say, dull—gentleman.

We should not jump to conclusions for he tells us of his *galant* side himself: "I rather liked saying trite nothings to women and rendering them services that cost so little."[16] This side of our man we shall find again in his light sentimental works of *galanterie.* But he seems to want to see himself as a reasonable man, as when he notes: "I shall be direct: if I could create for myself a character, I should like to be the friend of almost all minds and the enemy of all hearts." But the proposition is eminently a conditional one, for in the very next entry he writes: "I like incomparably more to be tormented by the heart than by the mind."[17] Here arises that same natural division in his character, rationally comprehended, which we have already glimpsed in the basic contrast of his intellectual position between absolute and relative: the head and the heart. Thereby he seems so eminently right as the spokesman for the beginning of the century that will later produce Rousseau and Diderot; the heart and the head will remain the most important battle-ground of the century.

All that being said, however, it is still toward the reasonable family man that our judgment turns as we continue to read his *Pensées.* "What makes me like living at La Brède is that at La Brède my money seems to be under my feet. In Paris, it seems to be on my shoulder. In Paris I say to myself: 'Mustn't spend that.' In my country, I say: 'Why, you must spend all of it.' "[18] And as a landed gentleman, despite his love of scholarship, his distractedness, and his wife's constant help in business affairs, he must not be taken for an easy mark among his domestics.[19] But, as his interests transcend La Brède to encompass all of humanity, so, by his own confession, do his simple and warm sentiments of the family man transcend La Brède and Bordeaux and, even, France. In one of the rightly oft-quoted passages of the *Pensées,* here is perhaps our best portrait of the man—and not at all a "stupid" portrait: "If I knew something useful to me but harmful to my family, I should put it out of my mind. If I knew something useful to my family but not to my country, I should try to forget it. If I knew something useful to my country and harmful to Europe, or useful to Europe and harmful to the human race, I should consider it a crime."[20] That is how modern this reasonable home-body from Gascony could be; that is why after a lifetime of research and thought he finally wrote a reluctant *finis* to a great book that still influences our notions of civilized human existence.

III *Life*

Moi, je n'ai pour régime que de faire diète quand j'ai fait des excès, et de dormir quand j'ai veillé, et de ne prendre d'ennui ni par les chagrins, ni par le travail, ni par l'oisiveté.[21]

From 1689 until 1700, Charles-Louis de Secondat lives at La Brède, a growing boy like any other growing boy so far as we can know, with one brother and two sisters. At the age of seven, in 1696, he loses his mother. He is close to two cousins on his mother's side; indeed the three boys will be brought up together when the cousins, in 1698, lose their mother. The head of the family is his father's elder brother, Jean-Baptiste, Baron de Montesquieu; Charles-Louis has apparently respect for all his uncles, most of them, it will be remembered, in the Church. While still a child, he writes to his father begging him not to discuss with his uncles the reasons his father has for being unhappy with his son, for, says the young Charles-Louis, "I shall so conduct myself in the future that you will not need again to grant me such grace." [22]

In 1700, the family sends Charles-Louis, as well as his two cousins de Loyac, to preparatory school outside Paris. This is somewhat surprising, given the great distance of the school from Bordeaux and granted the fact that Bordeaux possessed colleges of some reputation. But it was the Oratorian Fathers' college at Juilly that the family chose, whether because it wanted neither Jesuit nor Jansenist education for the three boys, or because the college of Juilly was known to them for advanced pedagogical methods. The Oratorian Fathers had a reputation for being independent, non-conformist, and were suspected by some of Jansenist tendencies; all of this might have appealed to Charles-Louis' uncle, "the most just and liberal man of his time," who as *président à mortier* had not been overjoyed at the revocation of the Edict of Nantes. Little is known about Charles-Louis' years in college save that some fragments of verse written as a student there survive and that he made occasional trips to the capital for holidays. He returns to Bordeaux in September, 1705, having finished courses at Juilly, and studies law at the University of Bordeaux until August, 1708, when he receives his diploma in law and is admitted to the Bordeaux parlement as barrister. For the next years, precious little is known, except that from 1709 to 1713 he spends much time in Paris getting first-hand practical experience and coming to know Parisian society. Almost certainly his rich knowledge of Parisian vagaries—so much a part of *The Persian Letters*—comes from this period; indeed the first of those *Letters* was probably sketched in 1711.

He returns to Bordeaux to settle down in 1713. He is twenty-four years old when late in that year his father dies, leaving him nominal head of the family. In 1715 he finds a wife, a Protestant, daughter of a respectable but scarcely rich ex-lieutenant colonel. Jeanne Lartigue will serve him faithfully as help-meet the rest of his days, and, if not pretty as it is claimed, had a good head for business affairs, which her husband entrusted to her on his frequent absences. In the same year he becomes councillor or judge at the Bordeaux parlement. In 1716 his uncle dies, leaving him his lands, his title, and his office of *président à mortier*. Charles-Louis de Secondat has become Montesquieu.

Bordeaux, after the death of Louis XIV in 1715, had something like a renaissance of energy and activity. Montesquieu becomes a member of the Academy of Sciences and finds warm friendship and exchange of ideas among young Bordelais of good family, in particular with another *président*, Barbot; a rich correspondence between them was unfortunately destroyed, it is reported, during the Revolution. Montesquieu seems to be interested in everything: science as well as politics as well as local problems. From this period we have essays on Roman religion, on kidney function, suggestions as to national financial reform, a sketch for an ambitious study of the physical history of the earth, papers on the phenomenon of echo, on the transparency of bodies, and on gravity, as well as, somewhat later (in 1726), a justification as a wine-grower against new rulings on the planting of vines. The governor of Bordeaux will write at that time: "As milord Montesquieu has much wit, he does not hesitate to treat in paradox and he prides himself by using brilliant reasoning that it will be easy for him to prove the most absurd things. I beg you to relieve me of replying to his memoir [on planting additional vines] and having to joust with him: he has nothing better to do than exercise his wit; as for me, I have more serious concerns to occupy my time."[23] Certainly *intendant* Boucher had important things to do, but he should have guessed that Montesquieu was more than a wit; he had his vineyards (and his income) to protect. Also, for the past ten years he had been contributing papers that were more than witty on subjects that were more than interesting paradoxes. In short, however slight some of the papers read before the Academy, they give us valuable insight into the development of a serious mind. But perhaps Boucher's mistake is excusable. What the *intendant* could know of Montesquieu's works was limited to the two he had already published. And those two had given him the reputation of a witty member of his social circle—little more.

It would be unfair to compare them. In 1721 appeared *The Persian Letters,* that satiric collection of letters—half-novel, half-character sketch—that sold like hot cakes, made a *succès de scandale,* and was pregnant with things to come. In the next years the young author is welcomed in Paris at the salon of Madame de Lambert, at the château of the Duke of Bourbon at Chantilly, in the circle of the marquise de Prie at Belébat, meetings of more serious minds. And in 1725 he publishes again: this time, a *galant* novelette in the taste of the times which has little to commend it to posterity. The serious projects are still secret or still uncertain in Montesquieu's mind, although *The Persian Letters* should have forewarned the advised reader.

When he returns to Bordeaux and La Brède in 1725–26, it is to sell his *présidence à mortier,* and to arrange some bothersome legal matters like the planting of new vines and the clarification of a boundary between his property and that of a local commune.[24] But in a larger sense, it is to get back home, after the Paris years, and set out on a vocation still only vaguely sensed. It is, in short, to settle down and work. It was probably in 1727 that he began to foresee what would eventually become the architecture of the *Spirit of Laws.* In 1728 and 1729, he travels (with the nephew through marriage of the maréchal de Berwick —natural son of James II and friend of the Montesquieu family —Lord Waldegrave, ambassador of George II to the imperial court of Charles VI in Vienna) to Austria, then to Italy, Germany, and Holland. From there in 1729 he travels with Lord Chesterfield to England, where he stays until 1730. Too much importance cannot be attached to these travels. They form the catalyst that brings the intellectual stirrings of Montesquieu to precipitation. After them, his life-work will proceed steadily with a good sense of direction. Aside from that vital fact, they have left us with Montesquieu's own record of his journeying and a fascinating record it is. Here, however, there is a sad note to be made; the bulk of his comments on his English sojourn was destroyed irrevocably at a later date, after Montesquieu's death.

From the moment of his return to La Brède from England and except for occasional trips to Paris, Montesquieu devotes the rest of his life to his work. That work is finally clear to him; he tells us that before he discovered his own principles he was many times tempted to abandon it. But now he sees that his work is a study of government—not particular government at a particular moment—but government as an idea, or to put it in his own terms, those of his final title, the spirit behind all law. Yet as a trial essay, indeed as a necessary preliminary study—much as a painter might need—he will for the next years study in effect a particular government, or rather the government of a particular people during the life span of that people as a recognizable body politic. That his choice should fall on the Romans is no surprise. First of all, his readings had been preponderantly in that civilization: he commands Latin (he tells us that Greek is the hardest language in existence, although he knew it well). Then too, the very basic layer of law as dispensed by the parlements (in Bordeaux as elsewhere in the South of France) was Roman law. In 1734 appears *Considerations on the Causes of the Grandeur and Decadence of the Romans,* a history of Roman civilization from the beginnings until the last gasps of the Eastern Empire. Gibbon will write a fuller history as history; Montesquieu is interested in the over-all cycle of government as exemplified by the Romans. The Troglodytes he had invented theoretically for *The Persian Letters* now become an actual moment in history, where he can study the evolutions and mutations from chaos to republic to monarchy to despotism to chaos. To judge of the function of a particular law, the law must be comprehended in its historical context, in the particular moment of the history of a particular people. Who would understand the phenomenon of law must understand the history of the nation which made such and such a law. Montesquieu must therefore become historian, but history will remain his hand-maiden, not an end in itself. As scientific method knows so well, individual cases of matter (be it frog's legs, kidney tissue, or combinations of sulphur) must be studied before hypotheses can be made on legs, kidneys, and sulphur in general and as elements. Montesquieu, feeling his way all the while, is applying the same method to human science that his admired Descartes had already applied to natural science. Or, to put it another way, which comes first: the particular law or the form of government? When forms of government change, do laws change in tempo? Or do old laws subsist to the benefit or the detriment of new forms of government? Does a civilization create the laws it requires? or does a civilization decay when it abandons primitive laws? In short, is law a Platonic absolute, or a relative concomitant of government many times doomed to fall into obsolescence? These were the questions that Montesquieu hoped to illuminate as he studied the very clear rise and fall of a great people.

In Paris, Madame de Tencin (famous *salonnière*) calls Montesquieu "my little Roman" while others speak of the decadence of Montesquieu. But he will continue despite failing eyesight (that part of his "machine" was never good) and momentary discouragement until 1748, when *The Spirit of Laws* is published in Geneva and pirated almost immediately in many quarters, as was the eighteenth-century custom. As for all his other publications except *The Romans*, the lifework appears without name of author. Almost immediately, there are reactions, most of them critical—so critical that Montesquieu could scarcely believe his tired eyes. Of course the Jesuits attack the book, as do the Jansenists, as eventually the Sorbonne and Rome. The book is placed on the Index, despite Montesquieu's efforts, in 1751. But, more perplexing, many of the so-called *philosophes* and liberal minds (starting with that enigmatic old party, Voltaire) are less than satisfied with the work and, not understanding or not wanting to understand the author's method and intent, are displeased that Montesquieu had not made perfectly clear his preference for a government *not* monarchy and *not* Catholic. Needless to say, the Baron de Montesquieu, good French Catholic with Protestant history in the family, had never intended to do anything of the sort. In 1750, he replies to a great number of his critics with the *Defense of The Spirit of Laws* and with other replies and explanations of his work lasting into 1752. Continuing to be cruelly hurt by the reaction, he somehow eventually abandons the battle, although never, perhaps, entirely. "I said of the abbé Laporte who wrote against *The Laws*," he reports in the *Pensées*, "and only to get a few pieces of 24 sous from a bookseller: 'A man who disputes in order to clarify does not compromise himself with a man who disputes to live.'" [25] And perhaps there is a bitter reflection of all his enemies as he writes, again in the *Pensées:* "For 25 years I have been working on an 18-page book which will contain all we know about metaphysics and theology, and all that our moderns have forgotten in the immense volumes they have published on these sciences." [26]

In 1754, he writes, at the request of D'Alembert, an article for the *Encyclopédie*, "On Taste"; it will be published in 1756. And in 1755, suddenly, and far from home and family in Paris, he passes away at the age of sixty-six—his own brand of Catholic to the end despite the attempts of some particularly cantankerous *dévots* to make him denounce his life-work. Diderot, it is said, was the only writer and *philosophe* to walk in his funeral procession. Aware as he was of the value of his life-work, Montesquieu would not have been inordinately disillusioned at this unspectacular exit from the world. As he wrote to Maupertuis in 1746: "As for me, I don't know if it's something I owe to my physical or to my moral being, but my soul seizes upon everything. I was happy on my estate where I saw nothing but trees, and I was happy in Paris amidst that mass of men equal to the grains of sand in the sea: I ask nothing more from the earth except that she continue to turn on her axis." [27]

IV *Travels*

Ici les murailles parlent.[28]

It is certainly in the record of his travels that the reader best catches the portrait of this man for whom everything was interesting. Early in 1728, in the company of Lord Waldegrave, he sets out for Vienna. Of his stay there, we have important fragments: on the one hand, character sketches of court personalities in which his power of subtle analysis continues the very real talent he had in this direction, shown already in *The Persian*

Letters, making him a worthy follower in the tradition of La Bruyère and La Rochefoucauld; on the other, and more precious to our knowledge of his embryonic theories of state, general conclusions about government of which the following is a good sample:

> Everyone knows that, although the states of the Empire [i.e., The Austrian Empire] are sovereign states, they are nonetheless in a kind of dependency, one to the other, as if members of a same body; and the right they have to make laws is subordinated to the fundamental law that unites them. A prohibition of trade between two states is contradictory to the union of the two states, and it is inconceivable that the states refusing all manner of mutual benefit could belong to a same state. What would be the position of the Empire if each of its members were to pass a similar prohibition? [29]

The most complete record of his travels is to be found in a sometimes obscure manuscript entitled *The Journey from Gratz to The Hague.* Venice is the first important city visited and although Montesquieu attempts to see clearly into the changing republican-oligarchic politics of that place and is intrigued by the problems of interpretation involved, his final judgment of the gem of the Adriatic as a civilized city is low. What is so close to Montesquieu's heart, individual liberty, does indeed exist there; he is somewhat puritanically puzzled by its approximation to license.

> As for liberty, they enjoy a liberty which most proper people would not want: consorting in broad daylight with prostitutes, marrying them, skipping Lent and Easter, being entirely incognito and independent in their actions; that's their liberty. But one must feel uneasy about it: man is like a spring that works better the more it is compressed.[30]

He is, however, not blind to the economic role of the prostitute:

> You will notice that prostitutes are very useful to Venice: for it is they alone who can make the local young men spend money, and one must admit that merchants get money only from them.[31]

But license is not liberty and the Venetian experience will help to clarify for later important passages of the *Spirit,* his conflicting feelings about individual versus social liberties. Another entry, reflecting the state of things in Venice, helps him to understand the recurrent cycle from republic to despotism: "Jealousy of senators in ancient republics—I have never understood so clearly how the Roman people could adore Caesar so much." [32] Of course, he is aware of Venice's special position in the century, serving as melting-pot for the famous, and he speaks of important visits made to scholars and politicians, in particular reporting conversations with the count of Bonneval and with his own pet peeve, John Law, of the infamous system. But his final judgment as tourist, scholar, and Frenchman can best be summed up in this pithy notation: "Gorgi compared Venice to an old whore selling off her furniture." [33]

He passes next into the territory of Milan, is particularly impressed by the islands of Lago Maggiore and the art collections of Italian notables about which he speaks knowingly, testifying to serious meditation on the plastic arts in general. Difference in climate and condition of soil is of constant interest to him:

> He [Prince of Malfi] says food in Milan is much more nourishing than that of Germany or France: to be definitely noted; and that Germans who feed their horses Milanese oats as if they were in Germany kill almost all of them by overfeeding; that even the bread is more nourishing—thus, impossible to eat two big meals.[34]

From Milan to Sardinia, whose cloistered intimacy and backward isolationism are not made to please a citizen of the world. The following outcry is indicative of the continuing problem of individual freedom within the State:

> Not for anything, should I choose to be a subject of these petty princes! They all know what you are doing; they keep you always under their eye; they know your income to the penny and find ways to make you spend it if you have a lot; they send commissars to make you put in pasture what you have in vineyard [a sore point for our Gascon].[35]

Then on to Genoa and Lucca and this somewhat confusing entry catches the typical French tourist and the philosopher in the same breath:

Mme de Modène was very bored by the pretensions of Genovese ladies. . . . And I said that putting Genovese women on the same footing as French princesses was like putting bats on a level with eagles.[36]

But what really was the height of misunderstanding came when Mme de Modène saw the countess Guicciardini, wife of the Emperor's envoy, who was at sword's point with all the Genovese ladies. ". . . And I said that I should be very unhappy to have all men like myself or resembling each other, and that one traveled so as to see different manners and customs, and not to criticize them."[37]

Next, Tuscany and Florence where Montesquieu admits that Florentine Gothic is superior to all other and that Santa-Maria Novella, "even if in Gothic taste," is a very beautiful church. He complains that the English always rob everyone (especially the Italians) blind, but adds, with satisfaction, that in their forays on continental art, "they rarely steal anything good." After Florence, Rome. And here Montesquieu has so much to say that it is impossible to give a fair idea. He is filled with admiration for the wealth of art and discusses painting as the connoisseur that he is; Montesquieu might very well have added his own treatise on the esthetics of painting to the spate of such books in France in the eighteenth century. It would not have been the worst. The sojourn in Rome, ever flooded with foreigners, provides occasion for the following characteristic comparison:

One must relax more in Italy for the Italian likes his comfort more than the Frenchman and is softer. In the same way, the German is harder than the Frenchman. It seems to me, therefore, that the closer you get to the North, the tougher you find people; and the closer to the South, the softer the body and the mind more relaxed.[38]

Mme de Staël could not have said it better. But the general feeling of this sincere and obedient French Catholic concerning the home of the Papacy is scarcely a complimentary one. He records with obvious relish one of those irrepressible Roman witticisms: "S P Q R has been interpreted: *Sanno puttare queste Romane.*"[39]

In Naples, Montesquieu is particularly taken by the hold of superstition over the south of Italy: superstition or naiveté and, what goes inevitably with them, trickery. In this country without taste, where serious guides point out the spot on which Cicero used to say mass, he is intrigued for pages with the miraculous liquefaction of the blood of Saint Januarius. Not that he believes for a moment the miraculous aspect, for he is at pains to point out that the heat of the candles held by the priests in propitious position explains the liquefaction. Still, he is at greater pains to dismiss any notion of subterfuge on the part of the anointed. There is here a singular combination of critical doubt and simple piety which characterizes all of his comments on the Church. Saint Januarius' blood, although readily explicable in natural terms, does not expose charlatanry. But, on the other hand: "I don't know if we are obliged to believe that the Pope is infallible; but I am quite sure that it is not possible for the person of any pope to believe that dogma."[40] This vacillation is all the more interesting as we remember that the *Voyages* were never meant for publication and therefore represent Montesquieu's frank thought. Returning to Rome for an extended stay he visits the Papal States, going as far as Rimini where he is deceived by an apocryphal Latin inscription to Caesar. Following the Po valley, he passes by way of the Lago di Garda and Verona into the Austrian Tyrol and Bavaria.

The Alps hold no charm for him: we must leave them for the Romantics; and distances in this barren Germanic countryside seem to him interminable. He facetiously, but not totally so, adds: "I think that the Germans who think so little and, consequently, are never bored, fabricated such long leagues just for us."[41] He scarcely hides his contempt for the Bavarians: "il Bavarese, piu stupido di Germani," he writes proudly in his repolished Italian. From Munich he follows the Danube valley through Augsburg and Stuttgart to the Rhine. At Augsburg, echoing Voltaire's statement on England soon to appear, he notes: "The burghers of Augsburg are much happier than those of Ulm, Frankfurt and Nuremberg, for, as there are two religions and since the Magistracy is divided, if a man is badgered by one magistrate, he has recourse to the other."[42] Along the Rhine he is not amused by the favorite names Cat and Rat given to two Rhine fortifications, but he is rather fond of pumpernickel bread with butter, a fact that must have caused, by now, generations of future Frenchmen to shudder. He continues north to the territories of the King of Prussia, Hannover, Brunswick, Osnabrück, and thus into Holland. Montesquieu does not like Germany and his comments seem suddenly less penetrating; one must say, I think, that he has here forgotten his own rules for travel and has allowed his vision to be colored by the shock he feels at the obvious lack of French polish in all this simple and direct German countryside.

If he likes Germany little, he likes Holland even less. A nation of tradesmen, mad for money, and intent upon extracting the last penny from every tourist for any so-called service rendered. The natural polish of the aristocrat is ruffled by this nation without the law of social grace: "The Dutch have two kinds of kings: the burgomeisters who dole out all jobs. . . . The other kings are the rabble—the most insolent tyrant possible." [43] But aside from the crudity of the populace, he misses his notion of art (i.e., the Italian school) to the point of revising some of his ideas on Rome:

> Men are colossally stupid! I feel that I am more attached to my religion since I have seen Rome and the masterpieces of art in her churches. I am like those Lacedemonian chiefs who did not want to see Athens perish, because she had produced Sophocles and Euripides and because she was mother of so many fine minds.[44]

Stupid as he may judge such a feeling, he has little time for the Dutch masters; the subjects painted are too everyday, too detailed—he clearly misses the classical formula of gods, *putti*, and *galanterie*. In fine, the Dutch are too plodding and deliberate for the French élan:

> The character of the Dutch is that they need much time to be moved and made to feel they are in danger. But once you have put that into their heads, you cannot take it out, even after the danger is passed. . . . They are brains moved only by great blows, that see only by dint of absolute clarity.[45]

From The Hague, in October, 1729, Montesquieu leaves for England, on the yacht of Lord Chesterfield. Of the travel notes still left to us, the first comes to the point immediately: England —John Bull—Beef-Eaters: "The people of London eat much meat; this makes them very robust; but at the age of 40 to 45, they croak."[46] The streets of London are impossible, so dirty and so badly paved that one "makes out his last will" before taking a cab. Yet London is immediately to be put in contrast with Venice on the score of personal liberty. London *is* liberty and equality, the liberty of proper people; Venice is the liberty of prostitutes and Holland the liberty of the rabble. But one must not expect to find Paris in London ("Paris, a beautiful city with some ugly things; London, an ugly city with some lovely things"),[47] and one must not ask the English to like and dine foreigners "when they don't even like and feed themselves." ". . . In France," concludes Montesquieu, "I make friends with everyone; in England I make friends with nobody; in Italy I flatter everybody; in Germany, I drink with everybody."[48] And there we have Montesquieu's short course on Europe.

Some of Montesquieu's observations are otherwise startling in a man for whom the English constitution and guaranty of liberty will later be so admired. The English people, he says, esteem only money, not honor and virtue, and they would sell their liberty over and over again to the king; in like manner their ministers think only of carrying the day in Commons and otherwise would sell England to all the powers of the world. Yet his conclusion to these several pages on England makes his admiration clear:

> England is at the present time the most liberal country in the world and I except no republic. I call her free because the prince is not free to do any imaginable wrong to anyone because his power is watched and limited by an act [of Parliament]; but if Commons were to become all-powerful, its power would be limitless and dangerous because it would have at the same time the executive power whereas now the limitless power resides in the parliament and the king and the executive power in the king whose power is limited.
>
> Thus a good Englishman must try to defend his liberty equally against the king and the Commons.[49]

There is still a natural aristocratic bias here and the language is none too clear (*executive* did not exist before in the French language), but one of the key ideas of *The Spirit*, a separation of power, is already writ large.

There is more in the travel notes: memoirs on the mines of

Neu Sohl in Hungary and the mines of the Hartz mountains, additional reflections on Rome, Genoa, Florence, and the beginning of an essay on Gothic style in architecture. Particularly in the memoirs on mines we see the curiosity of the natural scientist at work; the longer passages on Rome and Florence are a veritable guide to painting. But in Montesquieu's case and in 1728, it is idle to make such divisions. As he tells us so well, his soul seizes upon everything. Men of the cut of Montesquieu, not yet calling themselves *philosophes,* were perhaps not the *uomo universale* of an earlier period, but they come very close to that ideal. A striking new departure (Machiavelli aside) that one might begin to discern in Montesquieu's own travel notes is that he added to a very real concern for the natural sciences and the humanities what we might call a social and political interest and this lies at the center, not the periphery, of his attention and observation. There is one glaring absence in Montesquieu's itinerary; this is not Russia, nor Sweden, nor Denmark, but rather Spain. There were no doubt good political reasons for discouraging travel to a country so close to Gascony, but one is nonetheless surprised that he never turned in that direction. The surprise attenuates and ceases when one reads Montesquieu's comments on that civilization in his *Pensées,* other work notes, and finally *The Spirit.* He has so little regard for the country that it might as well have been relegated to Barbary.

V *Intellectual Preparation*

> *J'ai pris la résolution de ne lire que de bons livres: celui qui les lit mauvais est semblable à un homme qui passe sa vie en mauvaise compagnie.*[50]

The most facile accusation that might be hurled against Montesquieu by a politician is, I suspect, that he got all he knew in books. There can be no defense or denial; except for his years as *président,* Montesquieu was involved in no active way with government. He is the intellectual par excellence: the ivory-tower scholar as opposed to the man of action. Of course he is not alone in this company: Rousseau's ideal was *dolce far niente,* Thoreau was not even a dog-catcher, and Marx never crossed from the British Museum to sit in Commons. But that does not change the facts: The *Spirit of Laws* is a seminal book born of books—and critical reflection.

It would be impossible in such short scope, and not a little demanding, possibly even tedious to the reader, to study his intellectual formation in detail. That there are affinities with other thinkers to be suggested and direct influence to be studied is patent when one consults the important comparative studies mentioned below.[51] For the moment, let us attempt only to suggest which were the potent influences on Montesquieu as he glimpsed, developed, and matured his theories on human law.

In the conclusion of the Preface to *The Spirit,* Montesquieu, mixing discreetly pride and humility, writes:

> If this work has some success, I shall owe much of it to the majesty of my subject; and yet I do not believe that I was totally lacking in genius. When I saw what so many other great men, in France, in England and in Germany, had written before me, I was full of admiration; but I did not lose courage: And I too am a painter, I said along with Correggio.[52]

What he does not say is that he owes much to Italian thinkers, and to Greek and Roman classics.

His knowledge of Aristotle and particularly of Plato[53] must be taken for granted. Indeed, his whole intellectual orientation will vacillate, and for some time, between two attractions: law as a natural absolute or Platonic idea, and law as a relative science of analysis. Particularly in his study of the *Romans,* but in fact throughout everything he writes, the presence of Roman and Greek historians and annalists is constant. There follows here a partial list of such sources, all of whom Montesquieu did not always use critically, but all of whom he knew well: Varro, Dionysius of Halicarnassus, Vegetius, Titus Livius, Sallust, Polybius, Appian, Florus, Cicero, Plutarch, Dion Cassius, Caesar, Tacitus, Suetonius, Seneca, Eutropius, Claudius Quadrigarius, Herodianus, Zosimus, Ammianus Marcellinus, Lactantius, Procopius, Jordanes, Priscus, Menander, the authors of *The Historia Augusta,* Constantine VII Porphyrogenetes. An impressive list indeed, one that might impress the most ardent of classical scholars. To the Classics must be added the Holy Scriptures and the Church

Fathers. Almost all of these texts were known in the original although some through commentators and exegetes.

Such a classical background—with or without solid direct grounding in the Scriptures—was the usual intellectual baggage of most scholars of the century, particularly most of the *philosophes.* Montesquieu had also drunk heavily at the spring of that numberless and sometimes obscure tribe of German scholars of the late sixteenth and seventeenth centuries. Certainly he knew at first hand Grotius and Pufendorf and very likely others, as well as their commentators. ("Those learned men in *-us* whose latinized names seem to have escaped . . . for our amusement" as Dedieu says). "I am grateful to Grotius and Pufendorf," writes Montesquieu, "for having carried out what a great portion of this [my] work required of me, and with an excellence of genius I should not have equalled." [54] Pufendorf's very title (*De jure naturae et gentium* [1672]), *On Natural and International Law,* might well have been the title of Montesquieu's first chapter; his ideas, in a sense, start from that premise.

The Italians not mentioned in Montesquieu's Preface are nonetheless ever present to his mind in his working notes. There is, first of all, Machiavelli, whom Montesquieu seems sometimes not to admire, but the parallel between *The Spirit* and passages of *Il Principe* and the *Discorsi* (particularly in the French translations) are obvious. One of the very key ideas of the *Spirit,* on the necessary return of a corrupt government to its principles for salvation, can be traced directly to the *Discorsi.*[55] It was very probably the English experience of Montesquieu that changed his mind about Machiavelli.[56] But while in Italy, he speaks about and comes to know at least two other important thinkers: G.-V. Gravina (1664–1718), author of *De Ortu et progressu juris civilis,* and Doria, whose *Vita civile* (1710) was recommended to Montesquieu by his Bordelais colleague and friend, Barbot, and who tells us that treatises of law must henceforward seek out the reason, the fundamental and interior cause of all laws. And while in Italy (at Venice), Montesquieu notes in his travel log that he must remember to buy in Naples the *Scienza nuova* of Vico.

The French writers that come first to mind in one's general impression of Montesquieu are—far from being political philosophers—literary figures. Given the importance of *The Spirit* in the Works, it must seem an exaggeration to insist upon the spiritual affinity between Montesquieu and the French maximists, La Bruyère and La Rochefoucauld. Yet a great part of the *Persian Letters* falls into that literary category and great wealth in this style lies everywhere in the *Pensées* and other intimate notations of Montesquieu. Montesquieu could be easily shown a master of the genre. But, more important, it is the frame of mind that casts its ideas in maxims and the disabused understanding of basic human nature as they inform *The Spirit* that matter to us here. Montesquieu sees law and government steadily through individual human nature; the literary tradition of the character sketch formed that unflagging vision. Descartes is, of course, vital to Montesquieu's whole method as is Malebranche to his view of man in Creation. Pierre Bayle is exceedingly important to him if only in a negative way, for if he could not finally accept Bayle's atheistic morality, he was clearly provoked to deep and consecutive thinking on the problem of law and ethics by that precursor of the whole enlightenment in France. Fénélon and Fontenelle certainly influenced him, Fontenelle in person. Among his contemporaries he knew Helvétius, D'Alembert reasonably well, and he knew about other French *philosophes* including Voltaire of whom he, like many others, was not too fond.[57]

As it has been pointed out so often, the role of English thought in his formation cannot be overstressed. Hobbes provides him immediately with the *bête noire* against whom he can react. John Locke, sometimes via the French explanations of Pierre Coste,[58] is quite naturally for him the giant among English thinkers. But there is Bolingbroke; there are Harrington, Shaftesbury, Algernon Sydney, Thomas Gordon, Mandeville, Clarke, Cumberland, Milton, and Swift. And later, David Hume and Warburton. The influence of Locke and Bolingbroke is particularly great and has been studied.[59] Shaftesbury, Montesquieu places with Plato, Montaigne, and Malebranche as one of the great poets. And Swift, aside from his satirical masterpieces, again by way of Pierre Coste, added much in the way of clarity to Montesquieu's comprehension of the English constitution.

All questions of formative influence are difficult ones and this discussion has only scraped the surface. What must be gathered is the veritably monstrous appetite of Montesquieu in his reading, him whose eyes grew successively weaker at the task. At various times throughout his life and up until the end, like any good bibliophile, he wrote himself notes as to written territory still to be discovered. Some of these notes given here without further discussion may help define the dimensions of the curiosity of Montesquieu, never frightened even by some of the arid stretches ahead.

Original books to be read: *Scriptura sacra,* Stanley, Diogenes Laertius, Mariana (*De Rege et Regis Institutione*), Machiavelli, Polyen, something of Calvin and Luther, *Hudibras,* Seneca, Pliny, Ptolemy, Pausanias, Photius, Bacon, Lucretius, Clarke, *History of Medicine* by Dr. Freind.

Buy: Harris *Collection of Travels:* Churchill *Collection* (particularly Italian and Spanish voyages); Bailip *Etymological Dictionary* (*of*) *English;* Chambers *Dictionnaire.*

Buy: Bracton, *De Legibus Angliae;* Fortescue, *De Legibus Angliae.*

For my system on liberty, I must compare it with other ancient republics, and therefore read Pausanias, . . . Reineccius, *De Republica Atheniensium,* examine the aristocracy of Marseille which was no doubt a wise one for it flourished a long time; the republic of Syracuse which was no doubt foolish for it lasted but a moment; Strabo, Bk IV which seems to me to apply to my system; Plutarch, *Life of Theseus* on the Athenian republic, Plutarch, *Life of Solon;* Xenophon, *Republic of Athens;* Julius Pollux, *Onomasticon, de Republica Atheniensi;* Kekermannus, *De Republica Atheniensium;* Sigonius, *De Republica Atheniensium;* Coringius, *Thesaurus Republicarum.*

The fodder to satisfy his mind was thus vast; the resultant residue perceptibly slighter as Montesquieu makes clear in a note made for *The Spirit:* "I had to read much, and make very little use of all I had read." [60]

CHAPTER 2

The Work

J'ai la maladie de faire des livres et d'en être honteux quand je les ai faits.[1]

I *Early Works*

Discourse upon Reception into the Academy of Bordeaux, 1716
Dissertation on Roman Policy as to Religion, 1716
Discourse upon Reconvening of the Academy of Bordeaux, 1717
In Praise of Sincerity, 1717
Discourse on the Cause of Echo, 1718
Discourse on the Function of the Kidneys, 1718
Project for a Physical History of the Earth, 1719
Discourse on Cause of Gravity in Bodies, 1720
Discourse on Cause of Transparency in Bodies, 1720
Observations on Natural History, 1721
Dialogue between Sylla and Eucrates read before Club de l'Entresol, 1723
Discourse on Occasion of Reconvening the Bordeaux Parlement, 1725
Treatise on Duty, (fragment), 1725
Discourse on the Motives that should Encourage us in the Sciences, 1725
On Respect and Reputation, 1725
Treatise on Duty, 1725
Discourse upon Acceptance into the French Academy, 1728

HERE are listed almost all of the works of Montesquieu while still active in the Bordeaux parlement and Academy of Sciences. They are, for the most part, the length of a typical paper read in public (4–15 pages). They have been listed here only for reference and to give some notion of the varied interests of Montesquieu as provincial notable. In a few cases, they merit the following short analyses.

Discourse on Motives that Should Encourage us in the Sciences

INTRODUCTION: The difference between civilized nations and savages is in the cultivation of arts and sciences. Case of American Indians. If a Descartes had preceded the Spanish and taught the natives one thing: viz. that the effects of nature are a series of laws and communications of movement, the Aztecs and Incas would never have succumbed to the Spanish. This simple philosophical principle was not available to them: that new things can be known and explained by past experience in natural science. The Indians possessed certain valuable artifacts but they took unknown Spanish techniques to be the effect of an invisible power. Civilized nations know that there will always be change and novelty; thus gunpowder and the telescope were an advantage to the discoverer only for a short time. Science cures us of destructive prejudices.

THE MOTIVES:

1. Interior satisfaction at growing and helping others to grow intellectually.
2. Curiosity to see how far man can go.
3. The hope of success and discovery.
4. Our own happiness; love of study is the only lasting passion. Physical desires and pleasures pass with age.
5. If we do not encourage the mind (Montesquieu says the soul) we fall into boredom and vegetate in empty search for past pleasures of the flesh. If we do, we are unmindful of growing old.
6. Social utility. The pure scientist must not resent his relative obscurity when applied science takes over his ideas.

CONCLUSION—ON THE BELLES-LETTRES.

Like science, literature and the humanities constitute a pleasure in themselves and are therefore worth the candle. Ideas must be gracefully dressed to survive; thus science and belles-lettres touch. Malebranche would be unknown without his style; most people know all they know of Descartes through Fontenelle's graceful exposition of his ideas. Serious ideas can be clothed in light, even witty style. Apart from these considerations, such pursuits feed the spirit and keep men from debauch, slander, idle gaming, and excessive ambition.

REMARKS: The spirit of the eighteenth century is beautifully exposed in this short piece. Especially in the insistence upon the marriage of style and ideas, literature and science, grace and knowledge. And in the credo of progress: "Is it not a fine project to work so as to leave behind us men happier than we were?"

Dissertation on Roman Policy as to Religion

The Romans established religion neither from fear nor piety but because religion is necessary to every society. The Roman legislators, unlike others, made religion for the State, not the State for religion. They had no thought for moral conduct; they required only a fear of divinity in a fearless people so as to lead them at will. Nor did the successors of Numa think to *add* moral concerns to religion; that would have made the religion seem imperfect. So they brought about moral reform through new laws, for religion should be immutable. No religious text could be seen, no priest pronounce without prior permission of the civil authority. As Polybius saw, the strength of Roman religion lay in the superstition of the people who, being stupid, accepted the miraculous. If Roman religion had been more rational, the elite might have begun to believe it and thus have lost their hold over the people. Augury was used only when to the benefit of the commonwealth and as many victims were used as required for the correct (i.e., the civil authority's) prognostication. Examples of this manipulation. Religion was the most precious resource of policy and was arranged accordingly.

One must not believe the elite totally without religion. They believed in a sublime divinity of which the public manifestations were but a mechanical part. Thus the Stoic Balbus says that "God participates, by nature in all things—Ceres on earth, Neptune on the sea." The world soul, universally believed, could lend itself to all parts of the world. Thus is explained the spirit of tolerance of pagan religion: except for Egyptian religion, itself intolerant. For a long time the Romans confused the Jewish religion and Christianity with the Egyptian religion and treated them all accordingly. In Egypt the clergy was a body apart, a drawback to social unity.

The Romans blended all foreign divinities astutely into their own, without destroying the religion of captive nations. Having no other divinity in reality except the genius of the Republic, they paid no heed to the utter confusion of rival myths. The credulity of the people accepted anything.

REMARKS: If this rather disorderly, albeit learned, paper shows the immaturity of Montesquieu's mind and style, it also underlines a constant concern to illuminate the relation between Church and State. Although at this time, he probably saw parallels between Roman policy and French policy regarding religion, he will never attempt to undermine the position of the church in the French State as other *philosophes* were to do. This does not mean that he was without acute critical judgment of certain aspects of the Church (he deplored the treatment of Protestants, for example, as well as power politics among members of the clergy), but publicly—like the Romans—he accepted the basic Catholic divinity. One can foresee certain not yet aroused feelings he has for the masses.

II The Persian Letters

J'ai toujours vu que, pour réussir parfaitement bien dans le monde, il fallait avoir l'air sage et être fou.[2]

The Persian Letters, 1721—A novel written in 161 letters.

PLOT: Usbek, a Persian lord, can no longer live at the Persian court. To instruct himself in the ways of the world and escape the court, he travels with a young friend to the West.

Usbek and Rica correspond with friends in Persia, with other friends in Europe. Usbek, in particular, must keep in close touch with his seraglio. We get to know the different effects of Western civilization (particularly French) on the two Persians, the plight of harem women left alone and of their eunuchs attempting to preserve order there.

Usbek attempts to understand his own religion, government, and social existence, and he does this by contrasting them to French manners and mores. The letters break down into: story letters for the plot, philosophical letters, and a long series of character-sketch letters (close to satire in spirit) of the French.

Meanwhile, back at the harem, trouble grows apace. Usbek with Western women all about him, attempts to comprehend the logic of relations between the sexes. Become a philosopher in other matters—government, religion, social organization, and the like—he is incapable of making decisions about affairs of the heart. In the last letter, his favorite Roxane writes an impassioned declaration of independence ("I have recast your laws upon those of nature . . ."), and commits suicide.

The work is satire, a book of Characters like those of La Bruyère and Shaftesbury, a travelogue—but it is also a novel. In the many ideas pondered by Usbek as he is confronted by Western civilization, Montesquieu is already—unconsciously—preparing the great issues of the *Spirit of Laws*.

KEY PASSAGES:

Letter 3. Zachi, concubine, writes to Usbek revealing the effects of the absence of love, oriental style.

Letter 6. Usbek writes to a friend describing the singular feelings he now has at the absence of his harem ladies, at the absence of this peculiar kind of non-love.

Letter 7. Fatima, another harem inmate, writes to Usbek about the innate cruelty of masculine, possessive love.

Letter 9. The first eunuch writes to a younger servant traveling with Usbek, detailing the events and psychological anguish attendant upon his being made eunuch, then first-eunuch.

Letters 11–14. The Troglodytes. The most important sustained, philosophic discussion in the novel. Montesquieu sketches here for the first time his important discovery of the natural and historical cycle of governments. The parable supposes a tribe of cave-dwellers in Arabia, initially evil and totally without social order or responsibility. A foreign king attempts to correct them by force. They exterminate the royal family.

They elect several magistrates, but cannot bear them, and kill them.

They agree that there remains only a policy of every man for himself. Total chaos. The selfish winner today becomes the loser of tomorrow.

Now are discerned amidst the incomparably evil Troglodytes, two virtuous families who decide to live together. They multiply and flourish and their progeny live happily in a state of natural virtue, encouraged by wise customs.

Now come jealous neighboring tribes who covet the prosperity of the Troglodytes. But the virtuous families are ready to protect themselves and the unjust, stayed up only by their desire for booty, lose to the common cause of Justice.

The virtuous tribe grows to such proportions that its members find it advisable to choose a king. They agree on the most virtuous old man among them. He tries to evade their ambassadors to no avail. The parable ends with the tearful outcry of the chosen king: "O Troglodytes! Your virtue is beginning to weigh upon you. . . . You prefer to be subjects to a prince and obey his laws, for they are less restrictive than your customs."

The cycle has come full circle and one senses that the prince will, in the absence of individual responsibility in the citizenry, become despot, then tyrant.[3] There will be eventual revolt, disorder, small republic, large republic, monarchy; and again the cycle. The parable announces Montesquieu's theory of governments; there are three basic types: despotic, monarchic, and republican (the latter divided into oligarchy and democracy). Each government has come into existence and continues to exist because of a certain set of circumstances and therefore has a peculiar guiding principle. Virtue is the principle of republics and when it grows too burdensome to the citizens, the republic is corrupted and heading for the eternal cycle: chaos, order, chaos.

Letter 17. Usbek, in writing to his *mullah* advisor in philosophic and religious matters, attempts to explain rationally to himself varying customs as to cleanliness and uncleanliness. His tentative conclusion underlines the relativity of individual judgment, based as it is on sense data.

Letter 18. The *mullah's* reply to above. By way of a "revealed" myth, he attacks Usbek's conclusion and seems to explain everything. His final word: man cannot know everything, not even enough to question established religious practice.

Letter 24. Rica to a friend in Smyrna. First Persian judgment of Paris. Excellent satire touches on king, pope, and *Unigenitus* bull.

Letter 26. Usbek to his favorite Roxane in the seraglio. Letter congratulating Roxane on the good fortune she has to live under harem system and not in the loose manner of occidental women. Social satire.

Letter 28. Rica's satire on Parisian theater.

Letter 29. Rica attempts to understand organization of the Church and Inquisition. Daring (for the time) criticism under guise of Rica's pseudo-naïveté.

Letter 30. Rica on provincialism of the Parisian: "How can anyone be a Persian?"

Letters 32–34. Continuing views of Paris life by Rica and Usbek.

Letter 37. Usbek's portrait of Louis XIV.

Letter 38. Rica's conflicting views on freedom of women.

Letter 45. Rica gives portrait of an eccentric. The gullability of the Parisian.

Letter 46. Usbek on relativity of religious practice.

Letter 48. Usbek's long letter satirizing Parisian social life.

Letter 52. Western women.

Letter 60. Western Jews as seen by Usbek.

Letter 67. Long letter of Ibben (friend of Rica) containing the *hors d'oeuvre,* "Story of Aphéridon and Astarté," on religious intolerance in Persia.

Letter 69. Usbek on attributes of God and free will.

Letter 75. Usbek on the hypocrisy of Christians, in particular their ethics as regards slavery.

Letter 76. Usbek's controversial letter on suicide.

Letter 78. Rica's satirical letter on the Spanish character.

Letter 80. Usbek's important letter on types of government. "The government that leads men in the manner most appropriate to their leanings and inclinations is the most perfect."

Letter 83. Usbek on Justice, leaning toward a Platonic (transcendent) rather than immanent conception of God's justice.

Letter 85. Usbek on the utility of plural religions within a state.

Letter 89. Embarking upon a comparison of Persia and France, Usbek sketches what will become more clearly defined in *The Spirit* as the principles of three basic governments: despotism, monarchy, and republic.

Letter 92. Death of Louis XIV.

Letter 95. Usbek, in important letter, draws analogy between civil law and international law.

Letter 99. Rica on importance of fashion in Parisian life.

Letter 100. Rica on the patchwork-quilt quality of French legal tradition.

Letter 102. Usbek on some basic differences between despotism and monarchy.

Letter 103. Changing the law in the three types of government. Changes can be made only "by the prince (monarchy) or the people."

Letter 104. Usbek on the development of English constitutional law.

Letter 105. Rhedi to Usbek, pointing out limitations to the benefits of arts and science.

Letter 106. Usbek's rebuttal to Rhedi, justifying the arts and science.

Letter 107. Rica talks about the young Louis XV and the role of women in French government.

Letter 109. Rica on the Sorbonne.

Letter 112. Rhedi meditates on the depopulation of the world.

Letter 113. Usbek replies to Rhedi, conjecturing upon creation and durability of the universe in terms both of revelation and materialism.

Letters 114–122. Usbek continues his answer to Rhedi (above) at great length, attempting to explain historically the development (or decadence) of various societies.

Letter 129. Usbek on the role of chance in law-making.

Letter 131. Rhedi on the historical explanation of the rise of republics.

Letters 133–137. Rica satirizes scholarly and literary production in France, in particular the commentators (e.g., of religious texts).
Letter 138. Rica on the violent changes of fortune in France under the Regency and Law's monetary system.
Letter 141. Rica, at the behest of a lady, gives a literary allegory of despotism versus gentleness in affairs of the heart in a harem.
Letter 142. Rica in sustained satire (via parable) of John Law's system.
Letter 143. Rica on the power of superstition and miracles.
Letters 147–161. The dénouement of the plot. Especially #161, Roxane's declaration of freedom, and suicide.

When one has finished reading *The Persian Letters,* it becomes reasonably clear that Persia has relatively little to do with the book. The Regency that followed upon Louis XIV's death has much more to do with it. The intellectual climate of subsequent years has very much to do with it. The years between 1715 (the year of Louis XIV's death) and the publication of the *Letters* were characterized by political, moral, and economic confusion. Yet Paul Valéry, in a perceptive article on the *Letters* can reduce his comments almost entirely to an analysis of the Regency as one of the rare moments for literature when a whole civilization is in the throes of disintegration. "Europe," he says, "was then the best of all possible worlds; authority and ease shared a happy existence, truth still kept a certain measure; matter and energy did not govern directly—they did not yet rule. Science was still beautiful and the arts, delicate; there were remains of religion. There was enough of whimsy along with a sufficiency of rigor. . . . Even people in the street had manners." [4]

The Regency marked a crisis in French and, therefore, in European civilization. In these years of transition, beneath the deceptive ease of existence and laxity of morals, several major questions are being formulated, questions the remainder of the French eighteenth-century will try to solve.

For the modern reader, however, it is neither as a historical view of the Regency nor yet as an example of eighteenth-century comment on Persia that *The Persian Letters* should, and does, remain an important book. The letters divert and amuse, of course, as they were meant to do, but it is rather for ideas of continuing currency, validity, and development that the work remains a landmark. These ideas are obviously related to Montesquieu's subsequent (more substantial, less literary) works, *Considerations on the Greatness and Decline of the Romans* and *The Spirit of Laws.* Studies on these matters are not lacking.[5] But in a more general way, and apart from Montesquieu's own later works, there are in *The Persian Letters* three areas of thought which might be labeled philosophic ideas, social ideas, and literary ideas.

The *Letters* represent an excursion into comparison and contrast. Like some of his predecessors in the contemporary travel and voyage literature, Montesquieu is convinced that France, and Western civilization in general, must abandon insularity and ill-justified complacency. Difficult as it might be for a *président à mortier,* and a Baron de Montesquieu, the end of absolute values is a fact. Other civilizations, other climes, have produced other solutions for the various aspects of individual and group existence. The proper study, then, is no longer *a priori* justification of the status quo, but rather the examination of undeniable facts about various individual and social solutions as they have existed and do exist. Thereafter, ideally, one may attempt to arrive at some new and limited statement of absolutes which will remain valid for all of human nature insofar as it can be known. Montesquieu's method, as it has often and rightly been pointed out, is singularly divided between frank empiricism and deductive rationalism, for which he has a natural predilection and nostalgia. Yet all of his writings, and particularly *The Spirit of Laws,* starting from its very title, can be explained only by that division.[6]

It is in his insistence upon the details necessary to the preparation of a philosophic synthesis that we can see the Montesquieu who has often been called a forefather of the social sciences. In *The Persian Letters* we find those delightful and instructive particulars—of love, of marriage, of ambition, of social motivation, of friendship, of eccentric mannerism—that in a later age will grow into the more scientific disciplines of anthropology, sociology, and the behavioral sciences in general. Consider Montesquieu's women. He is sometimes confused about the particular seraglio inmate whose personality interests him most; it is now

Zachi, now Zelis, now Roxane. The reader finishes the *Letters* with no very clear idea of the character development of its heroines, not sure if this usual novelistic concern was even present in the author's mind as he wrote. Yet Montesquieu presented more than a diverting picture of women as the simple and necessary vessel of men's desires and pleasures—a picture that would have been not at all unusual for his period and for many of the novels that were to follow. He is interested in the plight of his Roxanes—not solely as female animals nor yet as classic representatives of feminine virtue, but rather, as both of these. He is aware, that is, of his harem ladies as complete human beings possessing sensual appetites as well as intellectual and moral motivations. His insistence on the lot of the eunuch is more than a pretext for shocking and titillating the gay society of the Regency. The eunuch is more than the literary symbol for decadent virility which Valéry seems to suggest; he is a study in the character of the incomplete man. In much the same fashion, Condillac and Diderot later considered the whole man as the piecemeal addition of the attributes and data of the five senses. In short, by attention to the details of individual human reactions to a given situation, Montesquieu abandons any absolute of human behavior and attempts first to reach some understanding of the multiplicity of possible human solutions to human predicaments. One first knows men in the aggregate, then one attempts to generalize, if possible, on human needs and human aspirations. This frame of mind clearly lies behind Montesquieu's later distillation of human laws (in the *Spirit*) and provides the motivating force for all the attempts to recapture the primary facts about "natural" man which characterize the rest of the century up to and after Rousseau.

The social and philosophic ideas of *The Persian Letters* have been treated many times;[7] the book is immediately susceptible to analysis of idea content. The literary value of the *Letters* has perhaps received less consideration. The book has been many times, and rightly, claimed as literature, but always in that peculiar manner of after-thought so often applied to all eighteenth-century French writing. It is a stereotype of non-French readers to pass off the century as rich in ideas and then to pose the inevitable question: Can ideas be literature? This is precisely what interests us here, just as it eventually interested Montesquieu.

Happily, Montesquieu has left, in the letters themselves, more than one hint as to the approach most likely to enlighten the reader on the literary aspects of the work—or rather, on the literary aspects of the work as Montesquieu saw them from within the eighteenth-century. Montesquieu himself was unable to speak of his early work except in a historical setting; his comments, written at a later date, bear the cachet of surprise of the man who has only later realized what he managed to write some thirty years earlier. Two things are immediately clear: Montesquieu was not impressed by the current novel as a literary form; he seems delighted that readers found in the *Letters*, "without expecting to, a kind of novel" ("Some Reflections on *The Persian Letters*"). If we can somehow square these seemingly divergent feelings of the author, we will be well on our way to a better grasp of the literary role of the work.

Seventeenth-century French literature was well known to Montesquieu. He was not, as too many suspect, completely lost in readings on philosophy, history, and law. The categories of that literature, in order of importance, might be given as theater, maxims, and fiction. Theater, with Corneille, Racine, Molière, and lesser lights, dominates the scene. That very special kind of literature—so French and so characteristic of the *salons*—the pithy truism, or maxim, is represented best by La Fontaine in poetry and by La Bruyère and La Rochefoucauld in prose. As a kind of tolerated outsider, there is the novel: pastoral and repetitious at the outset of the century, picaresque, realistic, and burlesque in reaction during the middle years, and finally, psychological and derivative of tragedy in works like Mme de Lafayette's *Princesse de Clèves*. The many memoirs and pseudo-memoirs written during the century were scarcely taken by contemporaries to be novels. On the contrary, they were popular precisely because they pretended to be true, and the memoir may be considered a fourth important genre.

Montesquieu has, of course, not written theater, but in many ways *The Persian Letters* fuse the other literary genres into something new, which even he seems surprised to realize has been taken as "a kind of novel." Consciously or unconsciously, Montesquieu used as ingredients in the letters: the maxim, or character portrait, familiar to antiquity and to French classicism (satire, as it were, in prose); the relation of anecdotes about known personalities which is the soul of the memoir; and, borrowing from novelists other than Mme de Lafayette, the exposition of obviously fictional characters tied loosely together by a sort of plot. And yet *The Persian Letters* does not properly fit into any one literary genre. There is no universal character; there are only characters observed by foreigners who never pretend that their behavior is universal. The element of memoir is more incidental than basic. There is not the usual loose extravagance with which the novels of the time awaited the consummation of love (even though, in the manner of Cervantes, there are three "hors d'oeuvre").

Montesquieu describes the kind of novel he thinks he wrote in "Some Reflections on *The Persian Letters.*" First, there is a plot, which holds the characters together. Then, because at the very moment of their presumed writing, the characters are caught up in a set of present circumstances, their passions are all the more real to the reader; in other words, this is not a historical novel in which an omniscient third person, the author, is retelling events after the fact. In the third paragraph of the reflections, Montesquieu is very clear. He has written an epistolary novel, which to his way of thinking has allowed him to mix together rationalization, or philosophy, and a story containing the emotions and passions of its characters. The plot has not, he says, been precast in his mind, and the whole agglomeration of elements seems free to move where it will although actually following a secret line of organization left obscure by the author. In another place in his writings, Montesquieu reduces this third paragraph to the sole importance of the epistolary form: "My *Persian Letters* taught how to write novels in letter form." [8] We must not underestimate Montesquieu's perception in singling out that form. But there is more than this behind the third paragraph, more perhaps than Montesquieu, with his attention shifted to a work of another nature, was aware of.

Montesquieu's realization that the epistolary novel could break the stereotype of the typical romance, could mix philosophy, politics, and ethics *as well as* plot line (although not seemingly preplotted) *and* the characters' passions caught in the quick, suggests a veiled awareness of a later, accepted notion of the novel. The surprise of Montesquieu's Persians at seeing a new world replaces the too obvious magic and extravagant element of past romances and yet provides the interest or amusement a reader looks for in the novel. In *The Persian Letters* the amusement is dependent, in part, on the satire of familiar things and places. The description of human feelings as they are being felt *in medias res* is the novelist's tribute to the sensationalists and the emotions —a tribute that looms large in the rest of the century. The random talk about philosophy, ethics, politics is the seemingly accidental intrusion of the complication of contemporary life and is in marked contrast to the stereotyped pattern of the usual romance that insists usually on love, or rather, the gradual conquest of love (a hangover from medieval romance via the Spanish pastoral). And the "secret and . . . obscure chain" of organization imposed by the author is what might be called the moral intent or central myth of the novel.[9] Let it be noted immediately, however, that moral does not mean moralizing and that the novel must remain essentially entertaining. The black overtones of a Dostoevsky or Kafka offer an immediate contrast to the gayer eighteenth-century conception of the novel. One of the few other comments Montesquieu later made about the *Letters* (*NRF*, I, p. 1244) was insistent on this point: "I venture to say that *The Persian Letters* was laughing and gay, and for that reason, was popular."

If we try to isolate the "secret and . . . obscure chain" or moral myth, around which the novel is organized (and Montesquieu seems to have encouraged such conjecture), we are immediately assailed by a crowd of ideas that at first glance seem to lack any unified organization. There is much obvious description of stock human passions straight out of seventeenth-century maxims—love, jealousy, ambition, pride, social artifice. Yet we soon become aware that these passions, individualized as they are, cannot constitute the chain of the novel. We also comprehend better a statement Montesquieu made elsewhere analyzing human reason into "moral reason" and "physical reason."[10] The latter suggests emotion and passion. Indeed as the author—who approved of *Manon,* despite the conduct of its heroine, because "love is a noble motive"—says in still another place, we must ridicule not passions but the manner in which they are handled, for "passions are not in themselves ridiculous." Our notion of the comic, he says, suffers precisely because we try to seek out the ridiculous side of passions rather than of manners.

Perhaps, then, the work is to be taken as a novel of manners. No reader of *The Persian Letters* could overlook the important role played by women. Is Montesquieu to be taken for a feminist? Are we to weep over the fate of the harem ladies? Hardly, with an author who admits (in a bad moment, probably) that "women are a very ridiculous sex." [11] But understanding and sympathy, we should have, and an objective (when possible) view of the whole changing phenomenon "woman." For if Montesquieu's Roman scholarship and his knowledge of past European literature made him conscious of the undoubted existence of a myth or ideal of womanhood, he now poses the question (and the wealth of specific detail of the Persian harem need not confuse us): What will happen when the ideal becomes the actual, when women, who were obedient while restricted by traditional literary conventional or harem walls, become free? Does the whole social organization collapse (as it seems to be doing in Usbek's seraglio)? Do we therefore float toward a kind of social and moral nihilism? Or perhaps a reversal and confusion of the sexes?

Again in the "Reflections," in what seems a routine justification and excuse for touching upon religious problems, Montesquieu has given the key to his "obscure chain." "The reader," he says, "is asked to be aware that the whole delight of the book consisted in the eternal contrast between real things and the unusual, new or strange ways in which those things are perceived." This is not the only delight of the book, but its organization as well.

In Letter XVII, Montesquieu plays with the idea (or prejudice) we have about a certain "real thing"—in this case, unclean meat. "It seems to me that objects in themselves are neither pure nor impure. . . . Mud appears dirty to us only because it wounds our vision or some other of our senses." It should not come as a surprise in the author of *The Spirit* that the first part of the central idea of the *Letters* is an obvious one: that all things, including "reality" itself, are subjective and relative—relative to time, to place, to climate, to religious belief, to racial and national prejudice, to intelligence. Following close upon this realization comes the necessary correlate: that sanity and civilization lie in accepting that relativity.

Such a unifying idea of *The Persian Letters* has certain elements in common with long-established scholarly views on Montesquieu's thinking in general. Gustave Lanson called the unifying principle of Montesquieu's work "historical determinism." Gilbert Chinard, in a careful article (taking the lukewarm reception of Montesquieu's *Spirit* by the *philosophes* as a point of departure) called it "historical pessimism." There can be no doubt that *The Persian Letters* represents much serious spadework, in source readings and in reflection, for Montesquieu's eventual philosophy of social man. Yet the terms determinism and pessimism seem somehow too grave for this work written at and about a period when everyone was young—irresponsible and perhaps reprehensible, but young.

"How can anyone be a Persian?" Montesquieu has a Parisian fop ask. And Valéry is right to take up the question and transform it into another, which involves Montesquieu's central myth: "How can anyone be himself?" That question, or one similar to it, is the "obscure chain" around which is organized the slim plot of two Persians in search of knowledge of the world. Much of the material involving Usbek and Rica is really autobiographical, involving Montesquieu. Such subjectivity is directly implied in Usbek's and Montesquieu's first step to wisdom. Montesquieu admits that he is like the classic traveler—the traveler whose thoughts upon watching strange countryside slide past, turn about questions like: What are all these people doing here? How can anyone live here? The first shock, then, is the realization of the tenuousness, the miracle of any social order. There are many travelers who will never recover from that shock; in the *Letters*, Usbek requires much more time to recover than Rica. Manifestly, some will never get over it and will react in one of two ways. Either they will retreat into a provincial shell of comforting traditional values, or they will remain precariously unattached, rootless, and withdrawn from all social reality because the initial shock of its relativity has swept the ground from under their feet.

What Montesquieu begins to glimpse here in terms of the novel is the possibility of a loosely organized genre in which the very precariousness of personal identity and social existence can be suggested in many different ways—by mixing philosophy, politics, and ethics, by portraying various finely drawn types, by showing the immediate (thus his predilection for the epistolary form) reaction of a given character to a given encounter at the very time it is happening, by piling up details with no obvious thesis or frame on which to place them. In a sense, "How can anyone be himself?" is answered by continuing to observe everyone being himself. There is no withdrawal in Montesquieu, and there is no reactionary retreat to familiar attitudes, however much such a step may have tempted the Baron de Montesquieu as he beheld with distaste and misgiving many of the details of Regency life. On the contrary, the realization of multiplicity in human attitudes only encouraged his study of human institutions.

The Persian Letters seems to have been written for that person (that is, each of us) who, shocked by the new and unusual ways of seeing what he took to be old, reliable reality, cries out painfully: "What! Is nothing sacred?" Montesquieu, as he views the excesses of the Regency, is not unfamiliar with that cry. His not too reassuring answer is simply that nothing is sacred, or at least, not as much as we assumed it to be. The next query—something like, "What are we, then, to do?"—is answered quite simply by his Persians' example, and by Montesquieu's own example. We live in the midst of the confusion, and we enjoy it. Then, if possible, we try to adapt to it and to accept it provisionally while we seek ways and means to extract from it a new synthesis, one that will respond to an inner principle or reality of the society, the time, and the place. Rome fell, says Montesquieu, because the Romans deserted their "inner principle." In any case, like the seasoned traveler in a foreign country, we must realize that social order is ever in the process of being remade, always a short distance from anarchy.

The episode of the Troglodytes is instructive. Social existence is cyclical and never constant. If Montesquieu at first thought natural virtue (contrary to Hobbes' state of war) was the regulator of social order, he later realized that in other positions along the cycle, a more sophisticated and artificial form of virtue —honor—must take over the job of regulating. Eventually, in *The Spirit,* he developed changeable principles and ideals for the various positions through which social existence evolves. The literature of the preceding century was, as Montesquieu points out in his notes on literature, a reflection and analysis of a particular, long-established stability; as such, it fell into classical, established genres. The main types of human nature had already been portrayed, and writers came too late to improve on them. Literary subjects now had to be finer, subtler, that is to say, reconsidered under the unsettling light of a society in transition.

Thirty years after the publication of *The Persian Letters*, Montesquieu discovered that the "kind of novel" it represented is the ideal genre for comprehending the complexity of a society in the process of change. During a certain time, the epistolary form of novel continued in vogue, then it gave way before new forms dictated by other techniques. But the novel itself continued to be the genre of a society in transition. And the novel, because of Montesquieu's own experience with the public reaction to *The Persian Letters*—and not because of any deductive thinking applied to the genre—became for Montesquieu that literary work in prose which, unlike existing examples called novels or romances, could discuss ideas in an entertaining form and against a familiar background.

If this idea of the novel is uncomplicated and as yet imperfect, we should nonetheless not underestimate its importance and influence. Out of such thinking, in literary terms, will grow the favored eighteenth-century genre, the *conte philosophique*, a flood of epistolary novels, and eventually, the novel as we suppose it ought to be. Out of the ideas of *The Persian Letters* will come the more mature and more guarded *Spirit of the Laws*, as well as the eventual dimension of the *philosophes*' vision, and their *Encyclopédie*. Valéry does not exaggerate when he says: "This book is unbelievably daring." Rare would be the modern work that dared to deal with contemporary society as frankly as Montesquieu deals with Regency France. Still more rare would be the book that attempted to do so and managed at the same time to remain witty and light.

The whole picture now fits together. If we originally chose to discuss *The Persian Letters* in its philosophic, social, and literary aspects, it is clear that the single idea of the relativity of reality and the accompanying acceptance of a universal indeterminateness tie all of these aspects together. Even so, Montesquieu would have found eminently true Ernst Troeltsch's phrase: "The Absolute is in the relative, though not finally and fully in it." No reader should suppose that such a frame of mind remains constantly optimistic. Indeed, the contrary is true in Montesquieu, and causes some of his more zealously optimistic *philosophe* friends to view him with suspicion.

It is perhaps literarily that the central theme of *The Persian Letters* is clearest. The book talks about many things, but it talks a good deal about women and eunuchs. Montesquieu comes close to pinpointing the creative motif of the novel in a later reflection: "It seems that timidity is joined to avarice; thus, old men, eunuchs, women—all this comes from a weakness of soul." [12] Here the timeless and the historic aspects of the *Letters* merge into one. If ever there was a moment of timidity, weakness, and avarice, it was the Regency, and that is precisely why Montesquieu wrote a fiction to satirize it. Yet there is the clear suggestion that such a state of affairs is a recurring and universal moment in the lives of men. When the central symbol or myth of a civilization can no longer be accepted as its "inner principle," and when nothing has been done to provide it with a new myth closer to its reality, then that civilization is in grave danger. A strong, firmly established peak of French civilization had just disappeared, shaken by the weakening of its stabilizing myth. Montesquieu himself, almost against his objective judgment, continued to hold on to one aspect of an orderly moment: he remained a monarchist. But as for scientific inquiry, both pure and social, he saw the implications writ large.

As for literature, he saw (in a discussion of tragedy) that new circumstances, customs, and language must come to renew it. If the sole realization of relativity remains constant, then in all human affairs—arts and sciences, politics, social organization, religion—new myths or newly accepted social ideals must appear to stabilize and create, if only for a moment of history, before, as with the Troglodytes, a new cycle begins. *The Persian Letters* is an eminently transitional book, whether in terms of the Regency or in terms of every recurrent crisis in human affairs. Perhaps Valéry is right—for Montesquieu is contradictory on the matter—in saying that it is the period of transition and incipient decadence, and not the period of stability, that gives rise to rich literature, bathed in the illumination of the end. "The end—always sumptuous and voluptuous—of a political edifice is celebrated by an illumination in which everything people were afraid to use up before is spent."

For all this talk of crisis and transition, we must not forget the basic ingredient of gaiety that Montesquieu saw in his book, a gaiety of acceptance of the times "when the world was young." That he was a younger man when he wrote it does not blind the older scholar to appreciating the virtue of that gaiety. Conversely, we must not assume that because it was a young man's book the possibility of serious thinking at its center is precluded. As Montesquieu said in another context, and as remains true for all literature, all is in the manner. And the manner of *The Persian Letters* is gay and amusing in the best tradition of the century of Watteau, Fragonard, and Marivaux. This does not exclude a certain foreboding momentarily glimpsed, but it most certainly excludes moral preachment and prudish sensibility.

The success of *The Persian Letters* was immediate and prodigious—surprising, certainly, even to Montesquieu. As was usual, then and now, publishers outraced each other to get some sequel, any sequel, into print. "They went about," reports Montesquieu, "tugging at the sleeves of everyone they met, saying: 'Sir, I beg of you, make me some more *Persian Letters.*' " The success was not without serious criticism and Montesquieu, several years later, when he was eager for admission to the French Academy, could have wished at times that the *Letters* had never existed.[13] A proper *président à mortier*, a serious member of the Bordeaux Academy given to delivering learned papers on myriad subjects of serious scientific research, did not with total impunity publish a light fiction with such gaily scabrous overtones. Of course, there *were* the ideas, and they were dangerous even if placed in the mouths of babes and Persians. But, except for officialdom at the time of the French Academy elections, the criticism was predominantly aimed at the manner of the book. "If they knew who I was," says, in the Preface, Montesquieu, who did not print his name as author, "they would say: 'His book clashes with his character; he ought to use his time to better purpose. This is not worthy of a serious man.' "

But the gay salon society of Paris beckoned and the *président* was quite willing to be lionized for a few years. In particular, he was taken to the heart of that indestructible *salonnière*, Mme de Lambert, who at the age of seventy-four collected about her the cream of the intellectual cream. And within that group, important arbiter of contemporary literary taste, Montesquieu gave birth to his next work, *The Temple of Cnidus*—probably for the bright eyes of a particular lady of the group.

III The Temple of Cnidus

The Temple of Cnidus, 1725—Pastiche of classical sentimental romance.

It is dangerous to risk assuming the role of arbiter for the tastes of a past generation. The peculiar literary exercise of fabricating romances, in the style of Greek pastoral, was calculated to delight and titillate the easy, blasé entourage of the Duke of Bourbon at Chantilly and Bellébat. I cannot imagine that this work is calculated to draw the enthusiasm of many readers of the twentieth century. Still, it shows well a constant side of Montesquieu's character—almost libertine although far from debauch, attracted by *galant* innuendo although far from open license and smut. It is ample proof, too, that Montesquieu after the success of *The Persian Letters* sensed in himself a real talent for writing novels and wanted to try his hand again. There is little doubt that he might have developed the sensitivity to personal idiosyncrasy of character, the critical acumen, and the fine sense for situation into worthy tools of the novelist's technique. But the direction of the *Temple of Cnidus* was scarcely the right direction, and he himself knew it only too well once the deed was done and committed to impression. Printed without name of author, the work, after some false attribution, soon pointed unerringly to its rightful author. And people were saying, however much delighted by the pastiche, that you could "feel throughout that *galant* work, a young playboy" or that the author was "a wise old fox in matters of debauchery." [14] Montesquieu himself protested violently: "The truth is that I am not at all the author of *The Temple of Cnidus.*" [15] Then, fortunately, came the French Academy affair, his travels, and the final realization that his literary contribution lay in a totally different area.[16] Not that he will never again cede to the urge to be gay (for he will reprint *Cnidus* with a similar, much shorter, work, *Cephise et l'amour,* originally printed together in 1725, much later in 1742). Let us say simply that *The Temple of Cnidus* is of interest to us for what did not become the pattern of Montesquieu's thought and style.

Plot: Preface of the translator. Montesquieu pretends to have come by the work when a French ambassador to the Porte bought some old Greek manuscripts and returned with them to France. He plays with the idea of situating this particular work in the corpus of Greek literature. He has made the translation into French and he calls on the young and the ladies to judge of the excellence of his author.

Chant One: Evocation of Cnidus, favorite home of Venus. The charm of her palace there. She loves to watch the Cnidian girls in their joy and innocence. Evocation of myths of Venus and Adonis, Psyche and Amor, etc., as paintings in the temple of Venus. Unlike the prostitution at other temples of Venus, here at Cnidus she is worshipped only by the sighs of true love at the altars of Fidelity and Constancy. Lovers' vows made at the temple: one example of many—"O powerful goddess, give me the strength to hide yet a time my love for my shepherd so as to heighten the effort of the confession of it that I wish to make him." I [the hero of the piece] know whereof I speak. I came to Cnidus, saw Thémire, and loved her.

Chant Two: At Cnidus, Venus has her oracle of which she herself is priestess. She chastises lovers who are not pure in heart. Examples of this. To me, Venus spoke in praise of my devotion to Thémire and her cult.

Chant Three: At Cnidus there are sacred games. Among all the beauties who present themselves on these occasions [pages of examples, *ad infinitum*], one does not see Camille; it suffices for her that her Aristée loves her. All the gods are charmed by Thémire. As soon as she appears, Venus has eyes only for her.

Chant Four: While Thémire is busy at the cult of Venus, I met Aristée in the woods. Tender Friendship between us. I was born at Sybaris where the Sybarites do not differentiate between voluptuousness and (biological) need. Effeminate men of Sybaris; the women "give themselves rather than surrender themselves." Love is but physical satisfaction. All delicious prior love play unknown. As soon as I was of age of reason, Sybaris disgusted me. Travels in all famous Greek isles in search of ideal. On Delos, finally, vision of Venus, who tells me to go to Cnidus. I arrive and, oh rapture! find Thémire.

Chant Five: I confessed my tender love to Aristée; he told me his sad story of which I shall not forget [unfortunately!] one word. Camille is the daughter of one of the important Cnidians; naturally, she is a vision of beauty. Perfect Camille needs no adornment, can be playful *and* serious. Aristée is love-sick [during two pages] for Camille who adores him and talks constantly of their love. She says: "Isn't it enough I love you?" And he says: "I should like you to commit for me a fault that love produces and that great love justifies." Aristée sighs and finishes his tale. Aristée is not happy.

Chant Six: While talking of their loves, Aristée and narrator become lost and enter a large field leading down a flowered path to a dreadful cave. Here they see Jealousy, Pallor, Sadness, and Silence. Further along is Fury. She hurls one of her snakes; it glides into their hearts. They abandon themselves to Fury. If Thémire and Camille had come then, the lads would have torn them asunder. Back in the daylight, they dream of their loved ones' infidelity. The hero proposes to Aristée that they go demolish the temple of Love, but it turns out to be Bacchus' temple and they are aware of their disorder and are calmed. They offer sacrifice to Bacchus. A group of bacchantes arrives with Pan, then Bacchus with Ariadne. Bacchanale led by Ariadne and Bacchus.

Chant Seven: They leave the temple of Bacchus and are again assailed by cruel tortures and doubts. They near the sacred oracle of Venus. They become separated in crowd. Aristée already in embrace with Camille. Hero finally finds Thémire; his jealousy rises. She has been mad with worry but Venus assures her he still loves her. Grand scene of pardon-seeking for the doubts of Jealousy. They wander into a woods; passing encounters with satyrs, nymphs, Apollo, Diana, etc. The hero finds his love where? on her lips, her breast, her feet and—after the final gasp of coy *galanterie* on both parts—where you think. Final sentences:

> "No," she said, "I am not so cruel as you; for I have never wanted your death, and you want to drag me into the night of the tomb." "Open those dying eyes, if you do not want mine to close forever." She embraced me: I received my favour, helas! without hope of becoming guilty.

Cephise and Cupid: More of the same, but only two pages long. The hero watches Cephise as she clips Cupid's wings. Cupid returns to his mother's breast to recuperate his forces. Cupid punishes Cephise by making her fickle.

"Cruel Cupid," says the lover, "it is I you punish through Cephise."

Comment: In the preface to the first edition of the *Temple of Cnidus,* Montesquieu tells us what he thought he was doing in that work. His comments are worth noting. If they do not entirely justify his misspent effort, they do tell us something of literary development in the century.

"The story of Aristée and Camille," he says, "is unusual in that it is solely a story of sentiment. . . . The object of the poem is to show that we are made happy by the heart's sentiments and not by pleasures of the senses; but that our happiness is never so pure as not to be troubled by accident." It is true that this analysis, later in the preface, loses some of its seriousness when Montesquieu, incorrigible wit and prankster, adds: "I first thought of putting the original [i.e., Greek] alongside the translation; but I was advised to make a separate edition of the text and await the learned notes an erudite scholar was preparing, and this will soon be ready for publication."

The literary novelty of these early years of the century is, precisely, sentiment. Montesquieu, in his insistence on sentiment as opposed to sensuality, is sensitive to literary taste. When some years later (1734) he writes in his private notebook:

> I have read today, 6 April 1734, *Manon Lescaut,* novel composed by Père Prévost. I am not astonished that this novel whose hero is a knave and whose heroine, a whore taken to the Salpétrière, should please [the public]; because all the bad actions of the hero, the chevalier des Grieux, are motivated by love, which is always a noble motive however low the actual conduct. Manon loves too; which pardons her for the rest of her character.[17]

he is commenting perceptively on literary tastes of his day and foreseeing an important literary development of the century. But *Manon* is not *The Temple of Cnidus* and Montesquieu was attempting to tackle sentiment by way of an artificial and precious pastiche of obsolescent taste. The Greek romance, the pastoral, is as surely going as the taste for Fragonard, Watteau, and Boucher—with their myriad mythological gods and chubby cherubs—is going. *Manon,* whatever else it is, is in the realistic, not the "literary" tradition. After *Manon* and Marivaux, will come Rousseau's sentimental *Héloise* and other novels situated in a recognizable world of men, not shepherds. Just so, after Boucher will come Greuze and, particularly, that master Chardin, whose sentiment is situated solidly in this world of reality.

Voyage to Paphos, 1727 (reprinted 1747). Work in the same style, traditionally attributed to Montesquieu. Probably written in the same general period as *Cnidus* and *Cephise,* it would presumably represent Montesquieu's last effort to contribute to his literary fame in this artificial genre.

IV A True Story

A True Story, ca. 1725–1730? Miraculous Tale, unpublished by Montesquieu. An oriental tale, entitled *Arsace and Isménie,* published separately after Montesquieu's death, was possibly a long episode to be intercalated into Part IV of the *True Story.*

The work is divided into five books or parts, each of considerable length. It is interesting and instructive, if only as a document, to show Montesquieu, the writer of literature, in the process of trying to fall upon his proper medium. The *True Story* remains a kind of catch-all or hodge-podge, but the various elements he weaves into it tells us much of literary tastes and of Montesquieu's intimation of the novel.

The work begins clearly in the picaresque vein—echoes of Lazarillo and Gil Blas—in India. Abruptly, after a few pages, Montesquieu has fallen upon his literary myth or vehicle: he will make his hero deathless and timeless by the device of granting him memory throughout a vast series of soul-transmigrations. There follows, for a time, what sounds very much like a *conte philosophique* as Voltaire was to write them. But soon, Montesquieu, one of whose fortes and predilections (as seen in *The Persian Letters*) was the character sketch, falls into a pattern of endless reincarnations, for each of which he makes an excursion into character sketch doubled with social criticism. The ill-fated Greek pastoral (à la *Cnidus*) is not totally missing from his mind as he invents ever new incarnations. One long episode (a eunuch in a seraglio) is an echo of episodes that had interested him so much in the *Persian Letters.* During part of one whole book, he imagines his hero as an incorporeal and spiritualized servant of numerous Spirits or Gods. Thereafter, he falls naturally into a pattern that might be characterized as "through history, ancient and modern, with an ageless critic." At this point, John Law again is taken over the coals, as he had been in the preface to the whole work. The probable intercalation of *Arsace and Isménie* partakes equally of the artificial pastoral, the Greek romance built on peripety of lovers, and the vagaries of fairy tales. The whole of the device is based upon the metempsychotic hero recounting his past to a friend, Ayesda, who has lent him money in his present incarnation.

The book is not without some brilliant passages and the device is a clever one, used before and since. But in the final analysis, the tale becomes monotonous and assumes the appearance of a book of characters to which incidents can be added *ad infinitum;* the literary device is not organization enough and the final impression is of a literary recreation for a writer in search of himself. It is therein that the work possesses some interest. For Montesquieu has clearly analyzed all the types of fiction that have passed for being a novel. He is, in his preface, even aware of the confusion in France from *ca.* 1680 until well into the eighteenth century between "true" (i.e., really pseudo) memoir and novel.[18] He senses the possibility of a new genre here and a rich literary vein. But he does not quite carry it off and clearly gives up all such romanesque experiment after his travels to devote himself to the real work of his life—i.e., *The Spirit of Laws.* Strangely enough, he had already had the success he seems here to be seeking—in *The Persian Letters.* He is aware of this himself only later in his life; he has written a novel. But that was the first and last. With a few different turnings in the quirks of fate (and they are not, after all, so unusual) the stereotype might have been not of the serious président who wrote a seminal work on government and law, but of a Montesquieu, novelist, rival of Rousseau and Fielding. But, then, that is why stereotypes are dangerous.

V Considerations . . . Romans

La liberté ne s'obtient que par des coups d'éclat,
mais se perd par une force insensible.[19]

Considerations on the Causes of the Grandeur and Decadence of the Romans, 1734—Study of the history of the Roman Empire from its beginning to the end of the Eastern Empire, in 23 chapters.

Commentators have long and rightly called this long study the preparation for *The Spirit of Laws.* Montesquieu sensed, upon return from his travels, that this pilot study in history was necessary for him who would know the *spirit* of law; if, eventually, his interest in things English was vital to the final shape of *The Spirit,* one cannot be unaware of the continuing fascination of the Romans for Montesquieu—one of his earliest fragments, dating from student days, was a project for an *Historia Romana.* The historian must precede the political scientist. The whole of the *Romans,* it can be said superficially, falls neatly between the Troglodytes of *The Persian Letters* and the first books of *The Spirit.* Rome once was nothing; then she rose steadily; then she descended just as steadily. For all of this there must be a reason and that reason is what Montesquieu will seek to illuminate as he passes in critical review all of Roman history.

Like the Troglodytes, the early republic of tough, warlike citizens will continue some time before they revolt. The maxim, the guiding *principle* of the founders, continue for a time in the republic; "at the birth of societies it is the republican leaders who make the institution; and thereafter it is the institution that forms the leaders of the republic." But eventually, as on the occasion of Tarquin's rape of Lucretia, there is revolt and revolution and Rome exists for a certain time as a republic without kings. Inside, republican virtue continues to assure individual liberty; outside, *virtú* [20] continues to add to the dimensions of the nation. There is built into the situation an inevitable outcome. Republics, as Montesquieu will say so clearly later, suffer from a self-regulated axiom touching upon greatness of size; up to a certain point, the republican principle is enough to keep the nation together; past a certain point of physical growth, the principle weakens and, as with the Troglodytes, virtue begins to weigh heavily on the individual citizen. Change is inescapable.

"Having deposed the kings, the Romans established annual consuls." The system carried them far, for a king's ambition eventually flags whereas changing consuls bring fresh ambition to the state. The ruling principle of the Roman state becomes therefore quite naturally a principle of continual war and conquest. There follows a chapter documented by references to Latin authors on the Roman art of war. After their victory over

Carthage, the Roman pattern is constant and secure: "little wars and great victories." After the victories, the policy became: "divide and keep in thralldom which looks like liberty." Kings and states finally accepted the boon of being "ally of Rome" as the lesser of evils, for as ally of Rome they had only Roman duplicity (erected into a system) to fear. "Thus Rome was not properly a monarchy, nor a republic, but the head of the body formed from all the peoples of the world." Rome took care *not* to impose general laws on the conquered: "in countries conquered by Germanic nations, power was in the hands of the vassals, the law in the hand of the prince: it was precisely the opposite with the Romans." [21]

But as Rome was conquering the universe, there was, and had been always, within its walls what Montesquieu calls a hidden war, like a silent volcano. After the kings and with military consulship, an aristocracy had grown up, aristocracy at once military and civil. Wishing to inculcate a continuing hate for kingship in the people (the masses), the patricians, unfortunately, developed in them a great love for liberty and were eventually forced to grant the masses all they wanted. This was the second great revolution, the plebeian triumph or victory of the tribunes. This was no irrevocable event but certainly foreseeable. "To put it succinctly," says Montesquieu, "a free government [which is to say, one always in ferment], cannot possibly maintain itself if incapable, by its own laws, of correction."

Chapter IX is entitled "Two Causes of the Fall of Rome." While Rome limited herself to Italy, every soldier was citizen and the senate could control generals and masses, despite their tribunes. But when the masses could give their favorites power outside of Rome, "the republic was lost." "And if the greatness of the Empire destroyed the republic, the greatness of the City destroyed it not any less." For Rome began to accord, first to few, then to many, the coveted title of Roman citizen. What had been natural party division within Rome becomes now indifferent disorder there, and "Whenever one sees everyone calm in a State calling itself republic, one can be sure that liberty is no longer there." The two causes are really part of one: "it was solely the great size of the republic that did the evil." "She lost her liberty because she finished her work too soon."

In the introduction of Epicureanism into Rome and the concomitant thirst for wealth and luxury, Montesquieu sees another reason for Roman corruption (Chapter X).[22]

Chapter XI analyzes the contributions of Sulla, Pompey, and Caesar to Roman corruption as they weakened military discipline and bought the adulation of the masses. After Caesar, says Montesquieu, ". . . . there happened what had never yet been seen: there were no more tyrants and yet there was no liberty; for the causes that had destroyed it still subsisted." All was ripe for Augustus and Tiberius. "Augustus had taken from the people the power of making laws and judging public crimes; but he had seemed to leave them the power of electing public officers. Tiberius . . . took even that away and gave it to the senate, which is to say, to himself." There follow all the others from Caligula to Antoninus and up to Probus (282 A.D.). "What was called a Roman empire, in that century, was a sort of irregular republic . . . in which the militia . . . makes and unmakes the civil officer . . . ; and perhaps it is a rather general rule that military government is, in certain ways, more republican than monarchic." For the military had been allowed to take control; Probus was killed by his troops.

In Chapter XVII, entitled "Changes in the State," Montesquieu discusses the reign of Constantine, who officially sanctioned the division of the empire. "In republican times," says Montesquieu, "the Roman people . . . had naturally to share tribute; that caused the senate . . . [finally] to give them grain for nothing." Under the monarchy the practice "continued against principles of monarchy"; it would have been difficult to change the custom. "But Constantine, founding a new city, established the practice without any good reason." All the gold and silver is centered in the East; the West steadily declines; and then came, under Valens (378 A.D.), the Goths. The Romans adopt new policies (Chapter XVIII) and bad ones; for having first started by paying the soldiers, they continue by paying off the enemy. Montesquieu expands: "The Romans came to lead all nations, not only by the art of war, but also by their prudence, wisdom, constancy, and love for glory and country. When under the emperors, all these virtues vanished, the military prowess remained . . . ; but, when corruption crept into the soldiery, they became prey to all nations." From here, through invasion of new hordes, religious confusion—first amongst the Christians, then against the Arabs—the fall of the West, the theocracy of the Eastern Empire, Montesquieu follows the history of those first virtuous Romans to the bitter end when the empire finished "like the Rhine, which is but a stream when it becomes lost in the ocean."

The Romans is, stylistically, much closer to the informal essay than to discursive historical analysis. The shade of Montaigne walks more readily throughout these pages than that of Ranke. However delightful to the reader the essay style (and Montesquieu is often at the height of his style here), it is not always extremely clear how his ideas on the Romans are to be conceived of as sustained analysis. In great part, this obscurity arises from a confusion between what might be called cause and occasion; Rome, Montesquieu seems to conclude at one point, "was destroyed because all the nations attacked her at once . . ." This is the occasion for the defeat; the cause (or causes) have been steadily suggested elsewhere. They are of the nature of principles for Montesquieu, not of events. But the reader of the *Romans* must be constantly on guard not to confuse principle and accident. Shackleton, quite rightly, sees an echo of Bolingbroke: ". . . in the greatest revolution of the greatest government of the world, losing the spirit of liberty was the cause and losing liberty was the effect." [23] Superficially, Montesquieu has been tracing a parallel picture of laws, on the one hand, and customs, personalities, physical conditions, and social psychology on the other. What he attempts to show constantly is that certain laws seemed, strangely, to subsist after Roman customs had changed. Not for long of course, for they had lost their force, or, better, they had lost their essential spirit or genius. Put another way, Montesquieu has been retracing (loosely) the cycle of the Troglodytes and, turning over Roman history from early kings to republic to despotic kings, to despots, to emperors, to despotic emperors, to chaos, he has shown that, as was not true for laws, the principles of these various governments had already perished when the particular revolutions that marked the change in type of government occurred. There were, of course, moments of an attempt to "return to principle," as he makes clear; otherwise Rome would not have lasted as long as she did. All in all, a rather clear preference declares itself, throughout this long history, for the republican form of government. But the set of circumstances (as in

Rome) does not always allow that government to survive; its determinants being changed and its principle weakened, it can *only* develop into something else (monarchy, empire, or despotism). "The republic being necessarily on its way to destruction, it was only a question of knowing how and by whom it was to be destroyed."

In short, it will suffice to study this nation, historically, to find certain hypotheses that clarify the spirit of all law and all government. Then, if one can carry along these same critical hypotheses and apply them with the same critical acumen to the history of all peoples (at least, in Montesquieu's case, as many as one can know or read about), comparing human passion in various situations and seeking out in events similar, not to say identical, causes—if one can continue to do all this, the next work (and after how many years!) will be *The Spirit of Laws.*[24]

VI Universal Monarchy

Reflections on Universal Monarchy, ca. 1734. Originally to have accompanied in print *The Romans.* Chapter XVI of this short work was in large part borrowed from a 1728 essay, "Considerations on the Wealth of Spain." Much of that chapter and of various other parts of the whole work, end up eventually in *The Spirit of Laws.*[25]

This essay, slight in dimension, is nonetheless vital to the development of Montesquieu's thought. The obsession with the threat of universal monarchy was constant in Montesquieu's mind and he must have known works of the close of the seventeenth century that discussed it in various ways. As to Spain, from *The Persian Letters* on, that civilization (although it infuriates him) elicits again and again his meditation and comment; what happened there is of universal significance for the human race. Most of the ideas of this essay will turn up, properly simmered, in *The Spirit;* importance of climate as determinant, the problem of liberty, the sheerly symbolic importance of gold and silver (particularly in Spain), size of state, Frankish feudalism as determinant of European governments, etc.

The master idea is a simple one, announced in the first paragraph. "There is a question to be put: if in the present state of Europe, there could arise a Nation, like the Romans, capable of possessing constant superiority over nations." Thus Montesquieu's concern is timely and a natural outgrowth of his work on the Romans. His answer seems equally simple. Such a thing is morally (he means eventually, physically) impossible due to change in military science, invention of new weapons, rapidity of international communication, and basic mutations in theories of international law. Spain (in the chapter devoted to her) is the proof that economic facts of life have undergone complete modification since the Romans. In a typical, pithy sentence at the close of his introductory section, Montesquieu says: "Formerly, we sought to raise armies to take them to fight in a given country. Nowadays, we are on the lookout for countries into which we can take our armies to fight."

Montesquieu distrusts the standing armies of European nations, among many other reasons because they are anachronistic. His fear of what might have been Spanish hegemony at the time when Charles V combined kingdom and empire is not lessened as he recalls the ambitions Louis XIV had along these same lines. He recalls, in recent personal experience, the attempts of Spanish policy to upset the Orleans regency. Speaking frankly of Louis XIV (too frankly to have allowed the book to be distributed in 1734) he says: "If he had succeeded, nothing could have been more disastrous to Europe, his former subjects, himself and his family. . . . he would have had to extend his forces and frontiers . . . Germany . . . the North would have arisen, all the neutral powers would have declared their positions and his Allies would have changed sides." Fortunately, Montesquieu did not live to know the Napoleonic and later German bids for universal monarchy. But that they did not succeed, eventually, adds credence to Montesquieu's notion that modern life does not permit such conquest so easily. But far above the physical and moral reasons given by Montesquieu there is another reason, pregnant with future significance, if only ideal, that he expresses succinctly in one of the sections (XVIII) of the essay:

> Europe is now only one Nation composed of several: France and England need the wealth of Muscovy and Poland just as one of their provinces needs the others; and the State that thinks it can increase its power by the destruction of its neighbor, usually is weakened along with the neighbor.

VII Essay on Causes . . .

Essay on the Causes that Can Affect Minds and Characters

Date uncertain but posterior to the writing of some portions of *The Spirit* and anterior to its publication. Divided into two sections: physical causes and moral causes, this essay might be called an essay in social psychology and, as such, preparation for an integral part of *The Spirit.* The introductory paragraph is instructive as to Montesquieu's method:

> These causes [physical] become less arbitrary as they have a more general effect. Thus we know better what gives a certain character to a nation than what gives a certain mind to an individual, what modifies a sex better than what affects a man, what forms the genius of societies who have embraced a particular sort of life better than the genius of a single person.

Call the method what one will, Montesquieu is here proceeding from the general to the specific, from the statistical to the sample, from the collective to the individual. A critic of human affairs might very well argue against Montesquieu that if we cannot know the mind of an individual Frenchman (e.g., Louis XIV or Charles De Gaulle), we shall never quite grasp the character of the French nation. His point here is, of course, obscured and incomplete: we can see large more easily than we can see small.

VIII The Spirit of Laws

> *Cela sera là, goûté, adopté peu à peu par les honnêtes gens . . .*
>
> —Vernet [26]

The Spirit of Laws, 1748—Major work, published originally in two volumes in –4° in Geneva, in six Parts, in 31 Books of unequal length, themselves composed of chapters of various length and number. The Books carry the following headings:

Part I: Book I—On Laws in General (3 chapters)
Book II—Of Laws Deriving Directly from the Nature of the Government (5 chapters)

Book III—Of the Principles of Free Governments (11 chapters)
Book IV—That Laws Relative to Education should be Relative to the Principles of Government (8 chapters)
Book V—That Laws passed by the Legislature should be Relative to the Principle of the Government (19 chapters)
Book VI—Consequences of the Principles of the Various Governments as concerns the Simplicity of Civil and Criminal Laws, Form of Sentence, and Establishment of Punishment (21 chapters)
Book VII—Consequences of the Different Principles of the Three Governments as concerns Sumptuary Laws, Luxury, and the Status of Women (17 chapters)
Book VIII—On the Corruption of Principles of the Three Governments (21 chapters)

Part II: Book IX—Laws in their Relation to Defensive Strength (10 chapters)
Book X—Laws in their Relation to Offensive Strength (17 chapters)
Book XI—Laws Establishing Political Liberty in their Relation to the Constitution (20 chapters)
Book XII—Laws establishing Political Liberty in their Relation to the Citizen (30 chapters)
Book XIII—On the Relation between Administration and Dimension of Public Taxation with Liberty (20 chapters)

Part III: Book XIV—Laws in their Relationship to the Nature of Climate (15 chapters)
Book XV—In what way Laws about Civil Slavery are related to Nature of Climate (19 chapters)
Book XVI—In what ways Laws about Domestic Slavery are related to Nature of Climate (16 chapters)
Book XVII—In what way Laws about Political Servitude are related to Nature of Climate (8 chapters)
Book XVIII—Laws in their Relation to Terrain (31 chapters)
Book XIX—Laws in their Relation to Principles forming the *General Spirit:* Manners and Customs of a Nation (27 chapters)

Part IV: Book XX—Laws in Relation to Commerce, considered as to its Nature and its Distinctions (23 chapters)
Book XXI—Laws in Relation to Commerce, considered in Light of its World Revolutions (23 chapters)
Book XXII—Laws in Relation to Use of Currency (22 chapters)
Book XXIII—Laws in Relation to the Number of Inhabitants (29 chapters)
Part V: Book XXIV—Laws in Relation, in each Country, to the Established Religion, considered as to its Cult and Itself (26 chapters)
Book XXV—Laws in Relation to the Establishment of Religion in each country: its Exterior Policy (15 chapters)
Book XXVI—Laws in Relation they should have to the Order of the Things they Decree (25 chapters)
Part VI: Book XXVII—Origin of and Revolutions in Roman Laws on Succession (1 chapter)
Book XXVIII—Origin of and Revolutions in Civil Laws in France (45 chapters)
Book XXIX—On the Manner of Writing Laws (19 chapters)
Book XXX—Theory of Frankish Feudal Laws in Relation to the Establishment of Monarchy (25 chapters)
Book XXXI—Theory of Frankish Feudal Laws in Relation to Revolutions in their Monarchy (34 chapters)

The table above is, of course, limited in value. For if we are to assume that we can grasp the pulse of the work by analyzing the contents, we must also observe that some books have 45 chapters and others, a single one. Moreover, within a given book, some chapters (for example Chapter 6 of Book XI on the English constitution) are major essays—many times transported whole and finished through Montesquieu's notebooks, and other chapters consist of a single sentence. What is more, the whole of Books XXX and XXXI is, realistically speaking, an *hors d'oeuvre* or, rather, an elaboration of one rather long chapter that has already served its purpose within the work (Chapter 22 of Book XVIII).[27] Again Montesquieu is writing social science in the manner of Montaigne and, although the modern reader may breathe a sigh of relief at such departure from some specimens of contemporary social science writing, still we must admit that Montesquieu's notion of organization was spotty, at best very special. Indeed, scholars have complained since 1748 that there simply is no order in this great and diffuse work. Montesquieu, after announcing the object of a given book, becomes involved with a particular aspect of that object, or falls into digressions of a personal nature, thus giving the book an impressionistic style, but making it difficult for his reader to follow his development of theme and thought. Some of the book headings are, themselves, long, involved, and obscure. Many times a chapter will be headed—"The continuation" or "the conclusion" of this or that idea; the reader wonders, quite rightly, whether that conclusion or continuation might not more properly have fallen in the same chapter, and whether Montesquieu did not organize according to the time he disposed of for sitting at his working table or according to his powers of concentration on a certain day before his vineyards called him from his library.

What we can know of the composition of *The Spirit* belies all such suspicion. The work was composed slowly, steadily, many times painfully, over such a period of time and with such revisions and recasting (as witnessed to by his personal papers) that we must accept the fact of serious organization.[28] For the moment, let it be said simply that Montesquieu, feeling his way in a veritable jungle of matter, for purposes never before seen, and sometimes seen through a glass only darkly by himself, imposed his own personal style upon the ordering of his thoughts. The very title of the work is significant here. For although the eighteenth century basked in long, circumstantial titles, Montesquieu's sets something of a record: *Of the Spirit of the Laws, or of the relationship laws ought to have with the Constitution of each government, with Customs, Climate, Religion, Commerce, etc. to which the author has added New Researches on Roman laws touching upon succession, on French laws and on Feudal laws.* The following brief analyses by book will, perhaps, clarify somewhat such a bold venture.

Notice and Preface by the Author:

Montesquieu chose as epigraph for the work the Latin inscription: *Prolem sine matre creatam*—Offspring created without mother. Many explanations have been forwarded, among which: (1) that France being without liberty had not nourished his efforts; (2) that Montesquieu replied thereby to a critic's reproach (Président Hénault) that the disorganized book was a collection of fine material elements; (3) that Montesquieu realized he had no precursor in his endeavors in this new field. It is the last explanation that seems most likely.

A notice written for later editions attempts to assuage those who were incensed to find that Montesquieu refused to call *virtue* a principle of monarchy. He attempts to mollify them by explaining that he means *political virtue.*

The original preface traces in a few paragraphs the years spent by the author on his project. Many times tempted to give it all up, he tells us, the discovery of his "principles" gave him courage to continue and see his work begin, grow, progress, and finish in the past twenty years. There are the usual disclaimers wise men made in eighteenth-century France: he means no disrespect to anyone and would not live elsewhere. As to his method: "I first examined men and believed that in that infinite diversity of laws and custom they were not guided solely by their fantasy." Then, positing his principles, he sees that a "particular law was linked with another law or dependent upon a more general one." As to his intent in making the long study, he would be the happiest of men if all citizens could love even more their country, if princes and leaders knew more about legislation, if all men would conquer prejudice ("I call prejudice . . . not what makes people ignorant of certain things but ignorant of themselves."), and if all men could practice "that general virtue which contains love of all men." Knowing what other great minds have wrought and sensing what he owes them, in conclusion, he believes that he is not totally without genius, nor his work without merit.

Book I: Laws in General

"Laws, in the broadest sense, are the *necessary relations* deriving from the *nature of things.*"

Therefore, every being has its laws: there are divine laws, material laws; superior intelligences have their laws, animals have their laws, men have their laws. Note the angel-beast situation of man.

Things, including laws, are not produced by blind fatality; there is, therefore, a prime reason. Before there were intelligent beings, they were possible; before anyone traced radii, they were equal; before laws were made, there was justice. Note the Platonic flavor of Montesquieu's reasoning here.

Man, an imperfect creature, has need of law on three scores: religious, moral, and political / civil.

The first of all laws are laws of nature. These are God, peace [contrast with Hobbes' natural law of war], self-preservation, sex, sociability.

Opposed to natural law are man's laws or positive laws. These may be divided into three categories: international law, political law, civil law. International law deals with peace and war; political law with the reunion of particular or individual strength (various methods of reunion); civil law deals with the reunion of wills. These latter two must conform to the *nature* and *principle* of political union; political laws form that union, civil laws maintain it. In addition, these laws must relate to several other things:

1. terrain
2. climate
3. kind of society (pastoral, industrial, etc.)
4. degree of liberty in constitution
5. religion
6. inclination of citizens
7. wealth
8. population
9. commerce
10. customs
11. manners

Moreover, there are mutual relationships among all of the above. Montesquieu has not separated civil and political laws in his discussion for he is after their *spirit,* not their details. International law is, unfortunately, not yet based on true principles.

Book II: Laws and the *Nature* of government

There are, and can be, three kinds of government: Republic, Monarchy, Despotism, defined as: government of people as whole or by a part of them; government of one person through established law; government by one person's fancy, without law.

The Republican government can be of two varieties: Democracy or Aristocracy. Long discussion and examples of these: first of democracy (chapter II), then of aristocracy (chapter III).

Monarchy has as source of power the prince but with intermediate, subordinate, and dependent channels of communication of that power. The most natural channel is the nobility, so that a fundamental maxim becomes: no monarch, no nobility; no nobility, no monarch.

The destruction of this maxim gives despotism. Despotism has no nobility, rather a vizir or deputy who serves at the pleasure of the despot, in his place, whilst the despot gives himself over to pleasure.

Book III: The *Principles* of the three governments

The nature of a government not to be confused with its principle, or guiding attribute. The principles derive *naturally* from the nature of each government. They are:

Democracy—Virtue
Aristocracy—Moderation
Monarchy—not Virtue but Honor. Virtue is to be taken in its *political* sense: "political virtue is moral virtue in the sense that it is directed toward the general and common weal."
Despotism—not Honor but Fear

The statement of the principles does not mean they always exist but that they ought to exist; otherwise the particular kind of government is imperfect.

Book IV: Education and Principle of Government

Since the principle is what maintains each government in a healthy state, all education in various governments should be planned and administered so as to aim toward, encourage, and reinforce the particular principle. There follows a discussion of past and present governments from this viewpoint, with explanation of seeming discrepancies.

Book V: Legislation and Principle of Government

As in education, so in all legislation, the principle forms legislation and legislation, in turn, reinforces the principle.

In a democracy, laws should encourage equality and frugality, in keeping with its principle: virtue or love of country. Also should be encouraged by law: ancient custom and law, senators appointed for life, the young subordinate to the old, women subjected to modesty and decency, citizen subordinate to civil officer, paternal authority preserved.

In an aristocracy, the elite should be neither too rich nor too poor, offices should not be hereditary, the prestige of office should not encourage social inequality nor unfair commercial advantage, conflict of interest should be discouraged, and everything done by legislation to secure justice for all.

In a monarchy, laws should encourage nobility, hereditary titles, landed privilege, rich commerce to satisfy desires of court and nobility, taxation for nobles in keeping with their offices—i.e., they must not be overworked. The monarch must be prompt to execute decrees, ever searching for excellence and rewarding it, ever encouraging glory.

Of despotism Montesquieu says, in a flight of pure imagination, in a one-sentence chapter (13): "When the Louisiana savages want fruit, they cut down the tree and gather the fruit; that is despotic government." The despot should preserve but distrust his army, so as to preserve himself; he is the state. His domestic servants and policy should be conciliated with civil servants and policy. Religion and superstition are useful. Succession depends on fantasy, not law. Despotism must encourage in subjects poverty with accompanying usury; arbitrariness in all things is the despot's best guide, just as ambition in others is his worst fear.

From all of this, vital questions are formed on the three governments:

1. Should laws encourage citizens to take government posts?
   Yes in a republic, no in a monarchy.
2. Is it a good maxim to ask a citizen to serve in the army at a rank lower than one he once held?
   Yes in a republic, no in a monarchy, of no consequence in a despotism.
3. Shall the same person hold civil and military office?
   Yes in a republic, no in a monarchy.
4. Shall offices be sold?
   No in despotism, yes in monarchy, no in a republic.
5. Do governments need censorship?
   Yes in a republic; no in monarchy and despotism.

Book VI: Principles and Criminal Law

What constitutes crime, processes of law and trial, punishment as befits crime, vary in the three governments. Discussion is based on historic examples. Among problems discussed: law of talion, corporal and financial sentences, children punished through father, clemency in a prince.

Book VII: The Three Principles: Luxury and Women

Luxury in the three governments; "republics end up in luxury; monarchies, in poverty." Feminine conduct and laws touching upon arrangement of marriage. "It is against reason and nature that women should rule in the household."

Book VIII: Corruption of the Principles

Each government's corruption begins almost always with the corruption of its principle.

Republic. Democracy has two excesses to avoid: inequality which leads to aristocracy; extreme equality which leads to despotism. The desire to be equal to all, even government officials, is the end of political virtue. "In the state of nature, men are clearly born equal; but they could not possibly remain so. Society causes them to lose their equality and they become equal again only under the law." [29]

Aristocracy. Corruption begins when the elite rules arbitrarily. When their power becomes hereditary, the aristocracy is lost. An aristocracy needs to react to an outside danger and should encourage the elite to feel the dangers and wearisomeness of public office rather than its delights.

Monarchy. Monarchy weakens when classes lose prerogatives and cities lose their privileges. "Monarchy is lost when the prince, referring everything to himself, reduces the whole state to his capital, the capital to his palace, and the whole court to his person." [30]

Despotism. Despotism is, by definition, corrupt. It is destroyed either by its interior vice or by accidents that destroy its principle, fear: e.g., insurrection.

The slightest change in constitution encourages the destruction of principle. There follow four chapters on the distinguishing properties of various governments:

Republic. A republic must be limited in physical area.
Monarchy. A monarchy must be middling great in area.
Despotism. The dispatch of decision and action must counteract the adverse condition of great size for the power must come from one man and his deputies must be accustomed to administer his arbitrary decrees.

Book IX: Laws and Defense

The dilemma: a small republic is destroyed from outside; a large republic is destroyed by natural inner vice. Solution: federated republic. Laws and observation of this government. This is a vital moment in Montesquieu's thought.

Despotic governments defend themselves by isolation, not federation. Purposeful desolation of frontier area.

Monarchies, unlike despotisms, preserved by frontier fortification.

Book X: Laws and Offensive Action

Offensive war controlled by international law.

Offensive war can be defensive in aim.

Laws and observations of rights of conqueror and conquered, accord with the nature of governments involved.

In conquest, it is not sufficient to leave the conquered nation its laws but also its customs, "because a people knows, loves and defends, always, its customs more than its laws."

Book XI: Political Liberty and Constitution

Long and important discussion of liberty. "Liberty is the right to do all the laws permit." [31]

"So as not to abuse power, things must be so disposed, that power limits power."

The vital center of this book is the long analysis of the British Constitution. There are three sorts of power: legislative, executive (international law), and executive-of-civil-law (judicial). The two chambers of England important for the tranquillity of the citizen; ". . . one will bind the other by the mutual right of restraint. Both will be bound by executive power, which, itself, will be bound by the legislative." The source of this political philosophy is Germanic in origin, according to Montesquieu, a favorite theory developed in the last books of *The Spirit.* Since all things perish, such a state (e.g., England) will perish "when the legislative power will be corrupted by the executive."

The rest of the book studies this ideal situation (which Montesquieu takes to be fact in England) in the ancient world, particularly Rome. The book ends with this ever valid note (chapter 20) to the reader: "I should like to seek out in all moderate governments that we know what is the distribution of the three powers, and thus calculate the degree of liberty which each enjoys. But one must not always so exhaust a subject as to leave nothing to the reader. It's not so much a matter of making [the reader] read but of making him think." [32]

Book XII: Laws and Political Liberty of the Citizen

Political liberty as to the citizen is measured in terms of the citizen's security or his feeling of security. This is in turn measured in terms of procedure of accusation against the citizen for the variety of crimes studied in the rest of the Book.

Book XIII: Liberty and Taxation

Good and bad taxation in the various governments and various methods of collecting taxes. Taxes are, essentially, paid for the guaranty of liberty and the privileges of the constitution.

Book XIV: Laws and Climate

Leaning on "scientific research" (a lamb's tongue: first warm, then frozen), and his usual historical observation, Montesquieu sees climate as one of the important determinants of law. A first basic difference between North and South; the Southerner is more sensual, the Northerner more cerebral. Climate can be shown to influence various laws: criminal, religious, political, dietary, etc.

Book XV: Laws, Slavery, and Climate

One of the most sustained discussions of *The Spirit.* "In a democracy, where all are equal, and in an aristocracy, where laws should operate to make everyone as equal as the nature of that government permits, slaves are against the spirit of the constitution." For, "the liberty of each citizen is part of public liberty." Montesquieu's true spirit and critical sense is especially apparent in the following famous paragraph:

I do not know if it is the mind or the heart that dictates this article to me. There is probably no climate on earth where free men cannot be encouraged to work. Because laws were badly made, lazy men were found; because these men were lazy, they were put into slavery.

Book XVI: Laws, Climate, and Domestic Slavery

Discussion of the role and status of women and of laws touching upon their freedom, marriage, and divorce under different climes and governments.

Book XVII: Laws, Climate, and Political Servitude

In general, Asia is a more natural ground for conquered peoples than Europe.

Book XVIII: Laws and Terrain

Fertility, pastoral and industrial, insular and mountainous, superstitious and religious, etc., as qualifiers of law.

Book XIX: Laws and the Principles Forming the "General Spirit"

The "general spirit," a concept long under development with Montesquieu, finds final definition and statement here (chapter 4): "Several things govern men: climate, religion, laws, maxims of government, examples of things past, customs, manners—out of all which is formed and results the general spirit."

In a given nation, as one of these determinants acts with so much more force, the others yield just so much. Nature and climate act almost alone among savages; manners govern the Chinese; laws tyrannize Japan; customs in times past gave the tone to Sparta; government maxims and ancient customs give it to Rome.

This general spirit should not be arbitrarily changed; all things cannot be summarily corrected. The Book then studies, in historical and present cultures, the ways in which laws follow (and should follow) the general spirit and, subsequently and conversely, the way in which laws may influence elements of the general spirit.

Book XX: Laws and Commerce

Montesquieu is in general an advocate of free commerce, yet not all nations are destined for it. Observations on kinds of commerce and nations that can benefit from it. Nobles in a monarchy, for example, are not apt for commerce; "it would be the route to destruction for the nobility without any benefit to commerce."

Book XXI: Law, Commerce, and Change

Changes, throughout history, of commercial aims, methods, and areas with corresponding effect on law, with particular reference to Rome, Spain, and the New World. Chapter 22 treats a favorite subject of Montesquieu—Spain and her undoing by unwise commerce and monetary systems based exclusively on precious metals.

Book XXII: Laws and Currency

"Money is a symbol representing the value of all merchandise." Montesquieu, building on this recurrent conviction, studies fluctuations in real and ideal currencies, in foreign exchange ("relative value is fixed by general esteem of business men, *not* . . . by order of the prince."). Historical analysis of Roman attitudes concerning currency, exchange, usury, public debt. Montesquieu does not agree that public debt should have no ceiling, nor that a state should owe itself—i.e., circulate paper money symbolic of public debt. True wealth is labor, not money.

Book XXIII: Laws and Population

Humans (unlike animals), for a variety of reasons, are not constantly fertile. Marriage is a result of the natural obligation of the sire to nourish his children. In civilized nations, offspring are assigned to the husband. Need for encouragement to propagate; Montesquieu is convinced that the world is being steadily depopulated since ancient times. The more marriages, the better; "the fewer married people, the less fidelity in marriage." On the question of charity: "A man is not poor because he has nothing, but because he does not work. . . . Whatever charity is given to the naked man of the streets does not fulfill the obligations of the State, which owes all citizens an assured subsistence, food, proper clothing, and a way of life in keeping with health."

Book XXIV: Law and Religion

An examination of religions *only* in terms of "political writer" not theologian. Rebuttal of Pierre Bayle (chapter 2) who held that atheism did not harm morals; "The question is not whether there are sometimes abuses of religion, but whether there is to be no religion at all among man." Moderate government best befits Christianity; despotism, Mohammedanism. Monarchy best accompanies Catholicism; republic, Protestantism. Second rebuttal of Bayle (chapter 6), who holds that Christianity could not create viable state. Bayle, says Montesquieu, confuses true religion with religious organizations. Interplay between law and religion. Religion's greatest virtue is to be *useful* to State; "[certain] dogmas were false, but they were very useful." Religion in terms of climate and custom; in general, religion should not be forcefully changed nor altered by proselytization.[33]

Book XXV: Law, Religion, and External Policy

Considerations touching upon organization of religions, particularly exterior to nation: clergy, religious orders, papacy, missions, tolerance. The high point of the Book (chapter 13), entitled "Humble Remonstrance to the Spanish . . . Inquisitors" is a magnificent example of Montesquieu's irony—and humanism.

Book XXVI: Laws and Their Objects

Montesquieu lists the different kinds of law: natural law, divine law, ecclesiastic (canon) law, international law, general political law, particular political law, law of conquest, civil law, domestic (family) law.

Important discussion follows on interplay between these laws and on the limits (restraining encroachment) of power of one kind of law over other. Important discussion of limits of canon and divine law over civil law; e.g., the Inquisition is illegal. Natural law, civil law, domestic law in marriage are treated. Chapter 18 gives a good example of difference between political and civil law. In general, each kind of law has its place and should not annex jurisdiction of another kind. This Book is vital to a comprehension of Montesquieu's thought.

Book XXVII: Roman Law on Succession

Historical analysis of subject. This one-chapter book is important in understanding Montesquieu's conception of his method. "We have seen," says Montesquieu, "that laws are related in myriad ways to myriad things. Studying jurisprudence is seeking out these relationships, and as the relationships change constantly, so are the laws continually modified. I think I cannot do anything better in the way of bringing this work to a close than to give an example. I chose Roman laws and I sought out those pertaining to succession. You will see through how many volitions and hazards they have passed. What I shall say of them will constitute a kind of method for those who would study law." [34]

Book XXVIII: On the Origin and Changes in French Law

The problem remains a vital concern of Montesquieu. In the longest book of the whole work, by way of historical analysis, Montesquieu attempts to assay the role in French law of each of its contributors: Roman law, canon law, and Teutonic (or Frankish) law. Montesquieu favors the overriding importance in French law of the last.

Book XXIX: Lawmaking

"I say now, and it seems I have written this work only to prove it: the legislator's spirit is a spirit of moderation." The burden of the book is that laws can be judged only within the general spirit that creates them: some seemingly stupid laws are good; laws that look the same are not always so and do not always have the same effect, sometimes the same law in two places has different motives and sometimes contrary laws have the same motive, etc. Laws must not be separated from their object, their circumstances—in short, from the general spirit. "Laws must not be subtle; they are made for people of common understanding: they are not an art of logic, but the simple reasoning of the father of a family."

Book XXX: Theory of Feudal Laws and their role in Establishment of the Monarchy

This book, although essential to Montesquieu's over-all plan, is an *hors d'oeuvre* or an addendum. In a controversy of the time, it was held: (1) that European monarchy had grown out of Roman law: (2) that it was a Germanic contribution and developed out of feudalism. Montesquieu held the latter view, strongly.

Book XXXI: Frankish Feudal Laws and changes in their Monarchy

Continuation of Book XXX. In reality, a history of Frankish establishment in France, the early dynasties and the derivation of political, social, civil, taxation and testamentary practices in French culture. One might see these final chapters as a work of preparation, never published: the counterpart for French laws of the earlier study on the Romans. Or, and perhaps more to the point, if the *Romans* help Montesquieu to see clear into his "method," then these concluding books of *The Spirit* are, in a sense, the successful application of that method after the long parturition of the *magnum opus* gave it final definition, and conviction.

IX *Contemporary Reaction*

The reaction to the publication was almost immediate. Within eighteen months, there were twenty-one editions, according to Flint. If from his good friends in Paris (Mme de Tencin, Helvétius, Mme Geoffrin) he received elated and sincere praise, serious criticism was not long in coming from several quarters.[35] Indeed, it soon came to appear that there was a concerted movement abroad to humble Montesquieu.

First, and perhaps naturally, there were the Jesuits. Montesquieu's acquaintance—friend is too strong—Père Castel,[36] had not received a copy; he was piqued, he was also therefore not able to review the book for the Jesuit organ, *Les Mémoires de Trévoux.* Montesquieu had preferred that he not review it. And so another Jesuit wrote the review (April, 1749) and took Montesquieu to task for many oversights and some downright anti-Christian attitudes: e.g., Montesquieu's treatment of celibacy and suicide, his suggestion that encouraging change of religion in a state was not advisable. He invited Montesquieu's answer to his criticism.

Later, the *fermier-général* Dupin (at the time, Jean-Jacques Rousseau's employer and host) wrote a book, certainly with Jesuit blessing, against *The Spirit;* copies (only a handful were ever printed) of this book did not however, for one reason or another, circulate.

Then a Jansenist joined the battle. The Abbé de la Roche, on October 9 and 16, 1749, wrote a strong criticism in the *Nouvelles ecclésiastiques.* Montesquieu's work, he says, is confused, disorganized, based on natural religion, Pope, and Spinoza (anathema to the eighteenth century), and, among other things, dares to find virtue unnecessary to a monarchy. The Abbé de La Porte joined in with criticism (in *Observations sur la littérature moderne*) in 1750. Although Montesquieu seemed to take things in his stride, he was disappointed and was busy preparing a *Defense* of his work which appeared in February, 1750.

The Defense of the "Spirit of Laws," 1750. This work of circumstance shows Montesquieu many times at his critical and witty best. He divides it into three parts: replies to general criticism; replies to specific criticism; reflections on the tone of criticism.

His strategy in the first part is to quote a passage of his critic and reply to it, sometimes extremely succinctly. Here are two particularly laconic examples:

Second Objection

Hereupon the author cites Plutarch, who says that law is the queen of all mortals and immortals. But is it from a pagan that, etc. . . . [*ad nauseam*].

Answer [*in toto*]

It is true that the author quoted Plutarch, who says that law is the queen of all mortals and immortals.

Fifth Objection

The author has followed the system of Pope's poem.

Answer

In the whole work there is not one word from Pope's system.

In general, Montesquieu's replies are serious and written after due consideration. But the tone is often delicious and unsubtly barbed, like the following: "The author of the *Spirit of Laws* is not at all a disciple of natural religion; but he could wish that his critic were a disciple of natural logic."

In the second part, Montesquieu meets specific and often lengthy criticism with equally specific and developed rejoinders. The burden throughout these criticisms is the same; the critics have simply misunderstood Montesquieu's whole method, and this is extremely revealing. They insist that Montesquieu is saying, about this and that, that such is what the state of things *should* be and yet he condones many questionable propositions. What they have not understood is that Montesquieu is reporting the nature of things, only very rarely expressing a preference. Thus his whole notion of relativity is bound to be misunderstood. Indeed the very pattern of relativity is anathema to the critics.

The third section is timeless; Montesquieu complains, rightly, that his critics are not criticizing the book he wrote, but rather accusing him for not having written the book *they* would have written. Montesquieu is perfectly aware that this work *sine matre*, has gone over the heads of most of his critics, and that the method he had so long sought and been so delighted to find (organization around his principles) is too novel for these men to grasp. His final paragraph is masterful: "It is with pleasure that I lay down my pen: I should have continued in silence if, from my silence, several people had not concluded I was reduced to it."

After the *Defense*, followed, at rapid rate, more attacks, thicker and more vitriolic. Montesquieu wrote a short *Clarification*, and a long *Replies and Explanations* for the Faculty of Theology. The polemics of the next years are too complicated to enter into here. The cruelest blow, against which Montesquieu did everything possible to protect himself, with the best of good will, was the placing of his life work on the *Index Librorum*. . . . by Rome in late 1751.[37]

Thus ends the story of a great book. Montesquieu will write yet a few more opuscules, among which should be mentioned the *Essay on Taste*, to appear in the *Encyclopédie* after his death. But his real work is finished with the *Spirit of Laws*. Since its publication, adverse critics have complained about the form of the long and rambling study: it totally lacks organization, so they say. Even those who are aware of Montesquieu's contribution to science and letters are hard put to counter the charge by revealing that organization in clear fashion. There can be little doubt that the first books are the most condensed ("I had to read much and make very little use of all I had read," says Montesquieu knowingly), the clearest, and perhaps the most important. Montesquieu has fit into them his constant meditation and the synthesis of a lifetime. Up to Book XX, or Part Four, granted the occasional digressions, the work develops steadily along the lines of the *plan* that Montesquieu had foreseen. There must have arrived, however, a moment when he despaired of ever finishing his readings, of imposing some order on the disparate mass of gleanings, and publishing his work before death or total blindness claimed him. Thus, in general, after Book XX, we seem to fall upon a series of opuscules or monographs that have not been fully reduced to their place in the larger work. Or, perhaps, for Montesquieu as for every writer (and all the more so as he was working in virgin territory) there was great and overriding reluctance to relegate too much of his painfully earned findings to oblivion. A great part of his thoughts *not* used for the *Spirit* are rich stuff indeed, and we should be quick to sense the loss of his notebooks. Yet to reduce is painful work and time lost from further inquiry; like Mme de Sévigné, Montesquieu did not think he had time enough to write a shorter work. In any case, we have in succession an essay on colonization, one on monetary systems, one on population, one on religion, one on Roman hereditary laws, and the last long essays on historical French law, feudal laws, and European monarchy. The two exceptions after Book XX are Book XXVI on the applicability of law, and Book XXIX on the legislator and the art of legislation. One senses that these two, probably in reverse order, might have made a fitting conclusion[38] to *The Spirit*, with the other material fitted into preceding chapters or books, and with the whole discussion of the Frankish feudal tradition transferred to a separate volume. But that was not to be; Montesquieu knew it was time to publish, complex as the final form may be. And that complex work cannot be commented upon adequately in a short space. Thus, the next chapter will attempt to clarify Montesquieu's thought in some depth, by topical or thematic arrangement.

CHAPTER 3

The Ideas

La loi, en général, est la raison humaine . . .[1]

I *Conception of Law*

INTO the first three chapters of Book I, Montesquieu has condensed a lifetime of thinking not so much on laws as on what law is. The exposition, the definitions in this section of the work, are admirably concentrated; one should not, however, be too surprised to discern there statements reflecting intellectual development during that lifetime.

Montesquieu, after some initial groping for his true subject, becomes increasingly aware that he is addressing himself to two basic problems: how to keep God (Justice) immutable as, more and more, his findings point to the truth of relativity in human affairs; how to apply scientific method (Descartes) to relative human affairs like law as well as it can be applied to the physical world. At the outset, there would seem to be a contradiction involved. This explains the continuing studies devoted to Montesquieu's "method" as a confusion or combination of inductive and deductive reasoning. It also explains Montesquieu's great predilection for Père Malebranche as the "poet" who had reconciled Christian faith and the scientific method—Malebranche, the Christian Spinoza; Malebranche, the harmonizer of Descartes and Pascal.

In those first pages of his long work, Montesquieu gives us the following definitions as to law:

1. Law is a necessary relationship that derives from the nature of things.
2. It is: a necessary relationship between Prime Reason and various beings (natural law);

   a necessary relationship between these various beings (positive law).

3. Natural law is related to God's wisdom and power.
4. Before man and his positive law, law had to be in relationship with Justice.
5. Natural law and positive law differ as the physical world and intellectual world differ.
6. Animals have natural law (feeling) but not positive law (knowledge).
7. (Positive?) Law, in general, is human reason insofar as it governs all the nations of earth.[2]

One need not long ponder this list before suspecting several superficial contradictions. If law derives from the nature of things, then (2) both Prime Reason and various beings are of the natural order of things. Natural law had to be comprehended by man through his reason; positive law is, by essence and before existence, related to Justice (God's wisdom and power). Yet positive law differs from natural law as the physical from the intellectual, or the immutable from the relative. "As an intellectual being, [man] violates constantly God's law and his own." Still, law is human reason, despite its variability, and, by essence, is Justice or God or Prime Reason. The easiest solution for the reader—a patent impossibility, seemingly—is to equate relativity with immutability; or natural-fallible with natural-infallible. The only other way out is, erroneously, to assume that natural law and positive law are different in essence, not only in degree, and that their *spirit* is different.

Montesquieu's thinking about the law is clearly in opposition to accepted terminology and Destutt de Tracy in his commentary on *The Spirit*, as late as 1819,[3] not unduly impressed by the fame of Montesquieu, puts his finger immediately on the difficulty: "A law is not a relationship and a relationship is not a law." One might quickly add that Montesquieu has clearly marked his work the spirit of the law and not the law, but his metaphysics still invites critics. The language he uses, no doubt, owes something to Malebranche and Samuel Clarke, as David Hume had early seen (1751) and as Shackleton so clearly shows.[4] But behind the language, one senses a radically different and, for an ex-président, legally unprofessional way of looking at laws.

As so often throughout this compendium abstracted from some direct experience but predominantly from readings in sources,

Montesquieu in this first book would seem to be collating all that has been said on the law into some complicated equation, cancelling out the common factors and contraries and arriving at some resultant, simple resolution that says as much as can be said before details, gradations, and degrees come to play upon the universal validity of that resolution. Thus, laws, in the *most general sense,* are the relationships between things (all things) as the nature of things shows: the nature of things seen, heard, read. God is not seen, heard, or read, but intuited; still, he must have his place, "first in importance," but not first in the order of the nature of things. Like Pascal with Descartes, one senses the danger grasped by Pascal in Cartesian theory and is tempted to apply to Montesquieu the suspicion that his God is first in importance as the *chiquenaude* or impulsion, but thereafter above and out of the nature of things that really interest Montesquieu. This would be unfair to Montesquieu, who clings to his Platonic conviction of the reality of Justice as absolute, all the while exposing justice cloaked under various cultures and climes. There is a confusion here between *a priori* and *a posteriori* and it cannot be explained away. What can be clarified is Montesquieu's basic problem suggested above: he *will* reconcile human affairs and scientific method.

But we have overlooked a key word kept by Montesquieu in his quintessential definition: laws are not only relationships, they are *necessary* relationships. Here arises the same obscurity: are they necessary (like the radii of a circle) because God made them so from all time, or are they necessary (like the radii of a circle) because they have been observed to be so and because no circle has yet been seen (or imagined) whose radii are not equal? One can only remark that the same ambiguity exists here between the Montesquieu who started his meditation on laws with Platonic predisposition and who ends his *Spirit* (as he had already ended *The Persian Letters*) with the conviction of relativity. To put it another way, the relationships are eventually, then, not necessary because God said they should be so by fiat, but because by observation, and in fact, they *are* so and no other way. This same frame of mind can apply as Montesquieu moves on to his discussion of natural law which indeed exists from all eternity but which is also empirically (however partially) observable by human reason.

It is true that Montesquieu seems to vacillate between "natural law" and "laws of nature" as expressions. It is also true that he defines laws of nature as those that derive solely from the constitution of *our* being—thus, animals purportedly would be without natural laws. In the final text he was a long time arriving at a definition basically so empiric. In his first thinking on natural law, he would seem to suggest laws engraved on man's intuition by God: i.e., those laws that "are the relationships between [Prime Reason] and different beings," in apparent counter-distinction to laws between beings.[5] Yet in Chapter 2, he insists on the "constitution of *our* being." That his thinking on the animal soul (that philosophic bone of contention since Descartes) has changed is evidenced by three paragraphs[6] on that subject still found in the manuscript but never printed in the text. In these paragraphs, and along with the closing paragraphs of Chapter 1 (except the last), it is evident that Montesquieu's introduction to his discussion of natural law was to be made by way of animals: "they have no positive laws since they are not united by knowledge," *but* "they have natural laws because they are united by feeling"—still, "they have with God no relationship more intimate than that of matter." Although Montesquieu does spare us the inevitable seventeenth-century discussion of pre-social man, he has not escaped, here again, a certain confusion between pre-social, eternal, God-given, Prime Reason principles (Justice); and universal laws, discerned by applying human reason to the facts of the human constitution, imagined pre-socially (justice).

Much has been written on the sources of Montesquieu's thought on these matters. The Latin legist Ulpian (170–228 A.D.) no doubt initially set his mind on animals; Grotius, Pufendorf, Malebranche, Domat, Clarke, Gravina, and possibly Vico provided source and sounding board for his precisions on natural law, in general. But the most constant scholarly preoccupation has been to assay the role of Descartes in Montesquieu's thinking, particularly in these first chapters which set the tone for the whole work. It can be safely said, I believe, (although not without some controversy) that however warm his respect for Descartes' method, and however great his desire to keep Descartes' deductive notions of eternal ideas (in Montesquieu's case, Justice), particularly during his first attempts to lay the metaphysics of *The Spirit*, Montesquieu simply does not remain Cartesian in the bulk of the work. The animals are perhaps the first temptation; the whole elaborate research into fact, thereafter, makes Montesquieu's empiricism something quite unlike the Descartes of the *Traité des Passions.* The intermediary of Malebranche is, no doubt, important, but that does not change the problem. One might say that Malebranche, proposing to reconcile Descartes to theology, salvages theology; and that Montesquieu, thinking to study laws *sub specie aeternitatis,* soon leaves both Malebranche and Descartes as he espouses empiricism, relativity, and the *science* of society.

It is also in his discussion of natural law that Montesquieu comes to grips directly with another seventeenth-century sage, Thomas Hobbes. After God (Montesquieu's first natural law in importance, last in order) comes the first by analysis of our constitution—the state of peace. Immediately, Hobbes, the theorist of the state of war, must be dealt with. Hobbes' idea of war, says Montesquieu, is a complex idea and therefore could not be man's first natural law; war is a social phenomenon and Montesquieu is operating, he tells us briefly and without explanation, in a pre-social moment. But Hobbes is, in the text, not so far from Montesquieu as many have thought. For Montesquieu, peace is the first law of nature: for Hobbes, man's *natural right* (*ius naturale*) is the liberty to use his own power; the first *natural law* (*lex naturalis*), reflecting the natural right, is in two parts—to seek peace and follow it, but when he cannot obtain it to seek and use war. Montesquieu's following natural laws are nourishment, sex, and society; Hobbes' second law is society and, directly thereafter (his list goes to twenty) come justice, gratitude, and complaisance. Hobbes, as Montesquieu has stated, is operating *after* the social contract not before, but their initial view of man, is not totally divergent.[7]

Once natural law is dispensed with (and Montesquieu had to start there for many reasons), one is on relatively clearer, empiric grounds with the positive laws. International law, political law, civil law: nothing could be more readily grasped from an examination of man's past. And when Montesquieu makes his famous statement that law (not otherwise identified) is human reason, one senses he is glad to be writing under the heading "positive law."

Now follows what might be taken as properly Montesquieu's basic theme of organization: nature and principle of government (here particularly Machiavelli's influence is felt) and then all the other determinants (the general spirit) where there are numerous precursors partially influencing Montesquieu. All of this, although not original, is Montesquieu's obvious contribution to his science of laws. But the foregoing difficulties cannot be, at this point, simply forgotten. Montesquieu's whole attraction to his subject (whether always completely conscious or not), his role in intellectual history, his genius, were involved precisely with seeing through both kinds of Nature (God's creation *naturata and* observable nature *naturans*), through metaphysics and science, through moral and physical causes, through Philosophy and History, through absolute and relative, through what ought to be and what is the spirit or guiding genius of human social life on this earth, its existence and its essence. If he seems more and more to underscore the relativity of that situation, this was not his primary intention nor his announced goal. It was simply his honesty and, seen in historical perspective, his great contribution to the Enlightenment and the Social Sciences.

II *Moral and Physical Philosophy*

In his *Pensées,* Montesquieu left notes (not used in his published works) on a problem of human determinism that must many times have ruffled his thoughts as he tried to grasp the general scheme of his *Spirit*. In his own terms, he attempts (probably *ca.* 1730) to come to grips with the part played in the formation of the man by physical and intellectual components; his terms will be moral reason (or causes) and physical reason, but it seems clear that moral includes for him here, the rational knowledge of good and evil. The first note merits quotation in its entirety:

> What causes most contradictions in Man is the fact that physical reason and moral reason are almost never in agreement. Moral reason ought to urge a young man to avarice, but physical reason turns him from it. Moral reason ought to encourage an old man to prodigality; physical reason urges him to avarice. Moral reason gives an old man strength and constancy; physical reason takes it [them] from him. Moral reason gives an old man contempt for life; physical reason makes it even more cherished by him. Moral reason ought to lend great value to the life of a young man; physical reason diminishes it. Moral reason

makes us envisage the torments of the other life as near; physical reason, by attaching us to all that is present, separates us from them.[8]

That this reflection on the relative roles of physical and moral causes was a constant one and a vital one to the eventual *Spirit* is borne out by the importance assigned in that work to what Montesquieu calls the general spirit (*l'esprit général*). This term, which so quickly and perhaps wrongly encourages us to contrast it to Rousseau's later *volonté générale,* was a difficult one for Montesquieu to fix; he keeps grasping at an important idea behind that term, he continues to add to or modify its definition. Suggested first in *The Persian Letters,* then in the *Pensées* (1731–33), then again there (*ca.* 1733–38), in the *Romans* (*NRF*, II, 203), in the *Essay on the Causes that can affect Minds and Characters,* he is preparing the final statement of the *esprit général* in *The Spirit.* The list of determinants is now, we must suppose, complete:

Several things govern men: climate, religion, laws, maxims of government, examples of things past, customs, manners . . .[9] If one were to attempt to assign these influences to Montesquieu's earlier dialogue on physical and moral causes, one might find it difficult to know precisely which cause is which. Of the many difficulties here, two are especially apparent: are there no other *causes* for Montesquieu and does the idea *moral* now subsume all non-material causes? Is there not a certain circularity in including in this list, that determines the spirit of laws, the laws themselves? Other problems come to mind immediately: what are *maxims* of government? what is comprehended under the vague term "things past"? and what is a good working distinction between customs and manners? To clarify somewhat this whole moral-physical axis in Montesquieu and to attempt to comment meaningfully on what many scholars have called Montesquieu's determinism or Montesquieu's pessimism, we must take a closer look at the essay on causes affecting the mind and character.

The *Essay on the Causes that can affect Minds and Characters* was written sometime before the publication of *The Spirit* (*ca.* 1736–43) and marks Montesquieu's penultimate treatment of this recurring moral-physical problem. He divides it clearly into two almost equal parts; physical causes and moral causes. The first part is a straightforward exposition of the influence of climate and the human "machine" on man: food, air, orography, prevailing winds, primary and secondary sexual characteristics, excessive indulgence, sleeping and fasting, etc. Each individual, from the physical point of view, is a special case of local climatic effect upon particular organs: this variety "is such that there have perhaps never been two men whose organic parts were in every respect equal." The state of the mind (it is clear that Montesquieu uses *esprit* here in that sense) is dependent upon an unbelievable number of determinants; it is not only the brain but "all the parts of the machine, often those we don't suspect" that determine it. Treating passions almost as physical causes, he shows that they have a marked influence on the organs; "some passions cause tension in our fibers, some relax them." The normal state for Montesquieu, one feels, would be a median position between tension and relaxation, yet he is aware that such a state rarely obtains: "great joy is a state as far from health as great sorrow. The pleasure of being [existing] is the only pleasure of a man at the moment of enjoying health." The last paragraph of this part is, incidentally, an excellent example of Montesquieu's wit. Speaking of a Spanish precursor in this field of climatology, he says: "The poor fellow looks for a reason why Jews' minds are more attuned to medicine than Christians' and he finds his explanation is the fact that the Israelites ate too much manna in the desert."

Part Two starts with a comparison between two men endowed with a reasoning mind: one in a barbaric, the other in a civilized nation. There can be no doubt that the civilized man will make greater progress; simply stated, the environment is the controlling factor, native mental equipment being equal. And so the whole of this moral section could have as its subtitle: the importance of education. Speaking of "incorrigible" barbaric peoples, Montesquieu gives us a valuable insight into his thinking in one short and otherwise pedestrian paragraph: "Brains thus abandoned lose their functioning: they almost completely lack enjoyment of their soul, nor does the soul enjoy its union with the body." Body is, of course, the physical machine described in Part One, brain (Montesquieu uses the physiological *cerveau*), we must suspect, is part of but not coterminous with mind (*esprit*), and the word soul (*âme*) must somehow be equatable with mind, although not totally so. He will use "soul" during the next paragraphs (e.g., the soul in the moment of physical love is closed to every other "emotion"). Then, in a significant paragraph he appears to revert to physical sensations, mixing them strangely with "moral" causes:

> Such is the physical constitution of our machine that we are too much affected or too little, by the things that come to us through our senses or through a certain sense, or from mathematical relationships or from moral, or from general conceptions or particular, from facts or from reasoning. One man will be convinced by rhetoric, another by simple logic. One will be affected by words, and the other only by evidence. One will never see the thing except with difficulty and will be uncertain; the other, finally, will see the difficulty better than the thing and will believe nothing. One will feel things and not connections, and will have no order; or else he will find connections everywhere, and he will be confused.

Montesquieu uses this passage to show that when, on top of all of these variations in human behavior, we have bad education, then all is lost. Thus, says Montesquieu, we have in actuality two educations: one (intellectual) from our teachers, one (social) from living in the world: one to train us to make decisions, the other, to please. A true man of parts reacts as the occasion demands; he sometimes *feels* what others (the school-educated) only *know*. "One might say that a stupid man lives only with his body; people of real parts (*esprit*) live only with the intellect."

What Montesquieu is suggesting here, I believe, is a comparison approaching the famous Pascalian division of the world between the intellectual mind and the artistic mind (*esprit de géométrie, esprit de finesse*), but he is far from being as clear as was Pascal. And the difficulty comes from a basic and continuing (at least, for a long time) struggle in Montesquieu's intellectual orientation between what we may call the experimental and the *a priori* rational, between the material and the spiritual. Many of his frank ideas (particularly in his personal notes: e.g., the *Pensées*)[10] sound—not accidentally—like the La Mettrie who would write in the late 1740's *Man the Machine,* no matter how shocked our *président* would have been to hear this. On the other hand, putting aside all that touches upon the superstitious, we must see that Montesquieu clings sincerely to a traditional religious conviction that suggests absolutes, and includes all of human life possibly qualifying as moral. The difficulty, for Montesquieu as for the modern reader, is simply that we can never be sure what is the part of the physical, and what of the moral. For when, in this essay so clearly marked, he would discuss the moral as opposed to the physical, the purely rational or intellectual fluctuations as opposed to climatic and organic variations, he seems to return again and again to physical causes. One can only conclude, I believe, by giving priority in Montesquieu's notions of causation and determinants in human nature to the physical and material—the climatic and organic. All those other *things* (and Montesquieu himself finds that word so useful)—religion, customs, manners, maxims, and laws, themselves the product of these—must have been thought of by him eventually as subjected to physical causes. And this, despite his own words (quoted in Dedieu, *Montesquieu*, p. 85, n.1): "One might say that the book, *The Spirit of Laws*, forms a perpetual triumph of the moral over climate, or rather, in general, over physical causes. . . . The entire work has scarcely any other objective than to establish the influence of moral causes."

But Montesquieu would not have understood our perplexity. In his own mind—as it is so clear in *The Spirit*—there is a gulf fixed between the material and the spiritual, between the physical and the metaphysical. That is why he needs to write the first few chapters attempting to lay a general or absolute basis to his study, a metaphysical definition as it were, although clearly marked as "deriving from the nature of things." That is why he insists upon calling his work *The Spirit* and not *Laws*. A great part of his genius arises from this insistence upon marrying two methods (the inductive and deductive), and two realms of human experience (the real and the ideal). That later social science, keeping only to his unconsciously preferred empirical method and prior concern with material data, could enlighten us on both the physical and spiritual aspects of human culture only makes his seemingly confused role more decisive. That some of his contemporaries saw what he could not or would not see in his *Spirit* explains the bitter attacks on his work by the forces of tradition and his adoption (although grudgingly) by the *philosophes*.

Thus we must read with care some of Montesquieu's important later passages in the *Essay on Causes*.

For there is in each nation a general character with which each particular character is more or less imbued. This is produced in two ways: by physical causes which depend on climate of which I shall say no more; and by moral causes, which are the combination of laws, of religion, or customs and manners, of that sort of emanation of the fashion of thinking, and of the air and stupidities of Court and Capital that permeate far.

Moral causes form the general character of a nation and determine the quality of its mind more than physical causes.

But as the good mind of these [peoples of the South—usually Catholic] finds itself by chance saddled with servitude, and the inferior mind of the others [peoples of the North—usually Protestant] leads consequently to liberty, it happens that slavery debases, burdens and destroys the mind whereas liberty forms it, elevates it and fortifies it. The moral cause destroys the physical cause, and Nature is so thoroughly deceived that the peoples she made to have a better mind have less sense (sensitivity), and those to whom she gave less sense, have a better mind.

We make for ourselves the mind we want and we are the true artisans of it.

It is not the mind that makes opinions, it is the heart.

If we read with requisite care the passages above (in great part centering upon North and South—a fact in itself enlightening, coming from the Catholic *président* of the South), we can illuminate further the hesitation seen above in Montesquieu's intellectual position. He has said (under physical causes) that Southerners are more relaxed and more sensitive, Northerners more taut, less sensitive. His first conclusion would seem to be: therefore Southerners are granted by Nature a finer set of circumstances for developing a fine mind. But, it is, in effect, Northerners who have developed the concept of liberty, thus using their minds to better purpose than the Southerners. However, in many ways, we make our own minds, and we make up our own minds, and, in that process, the heart is more important than the mind. Let us not stop here to attempt a difficult explanation of these seeming contradictions. The whole development, outlined in the passages cited, begs another question, perhaps more vital to Montesquieu's thought than the problem of physical-moral.

III *Reality versus Idealism*

If for physical reasons, the South *should* have the finer mind and if, in effect, the North seems to have arrived at liberty, then we can agree for the moment with Montesquieu that moral causes have outweighed physical. But, in the whole problem of education, and education for citizenship, it is clear that Montesquieu is underwriting what *ought* to take place against what does naturally take place: human nature must in a sense counter Nature to follow Nature (a position not too far from Hobbes' notion that peace should counter the basic natural right of war). Or, simply, that Montesquieu, much as he claims to be *exposing* the facts and the spirit of the laws, is actually *preferring* certain developments in law over others, a certain spirit of law over others. Which is to say, that the eternal of his first definition of law has become increasingly relative and that certain ways of seeing the relationships in the nature of things are superior to other ways of seeing those relationships. He will never say so clearly. We can sense his personal predilection for monarchy (on almost purely personal grounds), we know his admiration for republican virtue, and his contempt for despotism. The burden of his whole work, however, seems to be that these governments, developed by the nature of things, impose themselves naturally and that their principles and natures tend to preserve them until such time as that principle is corrupted. Yet, here, we feel the importance of an education (both formal and social) aimed at changing the state of things, at deriving benefits from constraint (North) not naturally existent in relaxation (South), at directing the spirit of laws toward a precise advantage, Liberty.

IV *Montesquieu's Conception of Political Liberty*

Montesquieu's thinking on liberty was like so much else in the *Spirit*, a lifetime process, moving through various developments, retrogressions, and affirmations. His original (and perhaps superficial) thought on the subject has the merit of not losing itself in interminable convolutions as concerns the absolute freedom of the will, or freedom of indifference. He is not too far removed from Hobbes ("Lastly, from the use of the word *free-will,* no liberty can be inferred of the will, desire, or inclination, but the liberty of the man; which consisteth in this, that he finds no stop in doing what he has the will, desire, or inclination to do.").[11] Montesquieu, in an early note in the *Pensées,* writes:

> . . . Moreover in free States, the masses are usually insolent. Do as one will there's never an hour in the day when a gentleman [*honnête*

homme] is not involved with the rabble and, great lord though one may be, one ends up involved always. In any case, I have little time either for the happiness of disputing furiously on affairs of State and never saying a hundred words without pronouncing liberty, or for the privilege of hating half of its citizens.[12]

Despite the satire, in *The Persian Letters,* on certain aspects of life in France, he is still, before his travels in Europe and particularly in England, content in his accepted notion of the superiority of monarchy in which liberty is, as with Hobbes, measurable in terms of the sovereign's order.

In Venice, he is struck by the—to him—apparent confusion between liberty and license: the Venetians seem pleased with their liberty to live with prostitutes. "But," says Montesquieu, "man must be restrained; he is like a spring that works better the more it is compressed." [13] We see this same conviction that liberty, far from being license, must exist *within* set bounds, in a comment written in Austria concerning sovereign or free states. "Everyone knows that, although the states of the Empire be sovereign, they are nevertheless in a kind of dependency with regard to each other, as members of a same body; and the right they have to make laws is subordinate to the fundamental law that unites them." [14] Yet he resents the excessive curiosity of petty princes and their invasion of private affairs as he passes through Torino. But it is, above all, in England that he begins to consolidate his personal ideas on liberty, and undergo the influence of English writers on the subject such as Locke and Bolingbroke. His entry for London is indicative: "In London, liberty and equality. The liberty of London is the liberty of gentlemen [*honnêtes gens*]," thus differing from the license of Venice: "The equality of London is also an equality of gentlemen whereby it differs from the liberty of Holland which is a liberty of the rabble." [15] Still, one feels here the ingrained prejudice of class that makes liberty a benefit *and* restraint of responsible gentlemen.

The first echo of a different attitude comes in another note on England: "The English no longer deserve their liberty. They sell it to the King; and if the King were to give it back to them, they would sell it him again." [16] The convictions of Hobbes begin to unsettle the prejudice of *président* Montesquieu. Yet England remains *the* free nation of the world because "the prince has power to do no wrong to any man because his power is controlled and limited by parliamentary act." For the first time in this note Montesquieu speaks of legislative and executive powers and concludes that: "A good Englishman must seek to defend his liberty equally against encroachments of crown and commons." But for all that, the statement is still tinctured by the frame of mind of a French nobleman who sees his class *between* those two forces of monarch and common people.

It is with the eleventh book of the *Spirit* that we come finally to a concentrated treatment of liberty—and here clearly marked *political liberty*. Therein, Chapter 2 reviews some of the myriad interpretations of liberty—political and otherwise—and merits quoting here in its entirety:

> There is no word that has received more varied meanings and struck minds so differently as the word liberty. Some took it for the ability to depose him to whom had been granted tyrannic power; others for the faculty of electing the man whom they should obey; still others, for the right to carry arms and exercise violence; and some for the privilege of being governed only by a man of their nation or by their own laws. A certain people has for some time taken liberty for the custom of wearing a long beard. Some others have attached this name to one form of government and have excluded others. Those who had had a taste of republican government put it in that form of government; those who had enjoyed monarchical government placed it in monarchy. In short, each man has called liberty the government that conformed to his customs and inclinations; and, as in a republic one does not have ever present, directly before one's eyes, the instruments of evil one complains of, and as even the laws in a republic seem to speak more of it and the executors of the law speak less, liberty is ordinarily placed in republics and excluded from monarchies. Finally, since in democracies the people seem to do about as they please, liberty was situated in this sort of government and popular power was confused with the liberty of the people.[17]

The bias in favor of monarchy would seem to continue in Montesquieu and the inherent fear of the mob to persevere, despite frequent admiration shown in the *Romans* for certain popular movements. Indeed, the tenor of this last sentence serves as transition for Chapter 3, in which Montesquieu gives finally his definition of political liberty:

It is true that in democracies the people seem to do as they please; but political liberty does not consist in doing what one pleases. In a State, which is to say in a society where there are laws, liberty can consist only in being able to do what one ought to want to do and in not being forced to do what one should not want to do.

Independence and liberty are two things, continues Montesquieu, liberty being what the laws permit, for if a citizen could do what they forbid, he would destroy his liberty since others could do the same. Political liberty, then, is that peace of mind arising from the opinion each man has of his security and, to produce such peace of mind, a government must be so constituted that one citizen cannot fear another. Perhaps he has best characterized his notion of liberty in a figurative idea (he excels in such style, but probably distrusts it) sketched twice in his notes but, unfortunately, not incorporated into *The Spirit.*

One of the ancients compared laws to spider webs that, having strength for stopping only flies, are broken by birds. I should compare good laws to those great nets in which fish are taken, yet they think they are free, and bad laws to those nets in which the fish are so crowded that they immediately feel caught.[18]

Whether or not Montesquieu seems to lean toward monarchy, this peace of mind becomes his essential definition of political liberty before moving on to an analysis of how best to encourage and preserve it. In Chapter 4, he makes clear that democracy and aristocracy are not free by nature since political liberty wants moderation: he seems to have forgotten, for the moment, that *moderation* was precisely the principle he had assigned only to aristocracy. But be a government moderate or not moderate, some machinery needs to be set up to insure the citizen's peace of mind against abuse of powers, abuse being a natural counterpart of power. And "to make abuse of power impossible, by the disposition of things, power must check power." Montesquieu is ready for the exposition of that constitution that will propose to do just this. Chapter 6 is, perhaps all too clearly, entitled "Of the English Constitution."

V *The Separation of Powers*

Montesquieu begins his chapter on the English constitution (Book XI, chapter 6) by reminding his reader of the basic kinds of power within a government. He will later alter slightly his initial description of these divisions. Of course, he is not completely innovating here; from Aristotle, not to mention a host of later writers, he could have quoted various analyses of branches of government. Aristotle had spoken of two basic branches, Locke, of three, but Montesquieu's trio will mark a new way of looking at the problem.

Whatever the glimmerings already in Montesquieu's mind earlier, it was the trip to England that, above all, helped to fix his ideas on the interplay of powers in government. And although the total experience there, his past readings in Hobbes, and his present acquaintance and readings of Bolingbroke became an undeniable part of his thinking (precise measurement being difficult or presumptuous),[19] it was, as has been clearly demonstrated, the influence of John Locke that is most verbally patent in Montesquieu's final casting of ideas in *The Spirit.*

Locke, in his second *Essay on Civil Government*[20] had mentioned three divisions of governmental powers, but they are perceptibly different from the divisions eventually analyzed by Montesquieu. Montesquieu's essays at divisions are, in reality, two, for his first mention of them does not correspond to the second. Shackleton has produced valuable evidence to show that the second definition (paragraph 6) of the three powers was, in effect, the earlier casting in Montesquieu's mind.[21] And Shackleton is, doubtless, correct in proposing that the later phrasing (which comes first in paragraph 1) owes much to Locke, as if Montesquieu felt the need of staying up his own ideas with an accepted authority. The language used by Montesquieu in this first analysis (particularly if one compares the text of the French translation) makes the influence of Locke obvious. It might be instructive, at this point, to outline briefly the major ideas of Locke so as to see more clearly, subsequently, the borrowings and innovations of Montesquieu.

Locke makes a tripartite division of powers into legislative, executive, and federative—the federative corresponding to what we should call "international relations." Thus, in effect, Locke distinguishes two powers, for, as he says, the federative and executive are almost always united. Indeed, one might say that Locke, operating under an apparent prejudice of monarchy (constitutional and liberal to be sure), is discussing three aspects of a single power rather than distinct compartments. As he puts it: ". . . thus the legislative and executive power *come often* [italics mine] to be separated"; they are not necessarily, or even preferably, separated. In fact, there is but one supreme power, to which the others are somehow subsidiary. "There can be but one supreme power, which is the legislative, to which all the rest are and must be subordinate"—except, of course, that this one power can devolve, where it came from, on to the people in case of neglect or fraud. From every page of Locke is reflected his basic predilection for the bourgeoisie (i.e., the propertied citizen) and, in the sense of that word before incorrigible abuse set in, for democracy. The reader of Montesquieu even before *The Spirit* will scarcely be surprised to learn that he does not share such predilection with Locke. Locke makes clear that the executive ought not to be placed in the legislative and that these two branches are in distinct hands "in all moderated monarchies and well-formed governments." As to a judicial branch, Locke says simply that every man is judge for himself (the people being deputer *and* discarder) and/or, of course, ultimately, that justice is in Heaven—"God in heaven is Judge." The ideal government (not spelled out by Locke) can, however, not remain static, for "things of this world are in so constant a flux that nothing remains long in the same state."

The all-important Chapter 6 of Book XI of Montesquieu can perhaps best be illuminated by the following schematic treatment. Parallels with and departures from Locke should be apparent.

Montesquieu's first division is into (1) legislative power, (2) executive power of things dependent on international law and (3) executive power of things dependent on civil law. The parallel with Locke in this late paragraph is obvious. But almost immediately (in the printed text) comes a clarification which is, this time, pure Montesquieu: legislative power, [simply] "executive" power, and the power of judgment. Very soon, although not immediately thereafter, Montesquieu makes clear that the legislative is to be taken as bicameral: commons and lords, so that one might almost speak of four (not three) distinct centers of power. The important things he has to say about each, in this concentrated and closely reasoned chapter (purporting to analyze the English Constitution), may be summarized as follows. For purposes of clarity that seem to take no excessive liberty with Montesquieu's thought, let us call these concentrations of power legislative, executive and judicial.

1. Legislative power:

   Power given to magistrates or permanent bodies since the general, not individual, will is concerned.

   Chosen locally and not specifically instructed on every matter by electorate.

   Chosen by universal suffrage except for the dregs of the population "reputed to be without any proper volition."

   If the "people" enter directly into legislation and execution, this is an abuse of legislative power. The people are too limited to legislate but capable of knowing a good representative. Under this sort of abuse—direct legislation by the people—the nation's elite would suffer.

   The executive must convoke the legislative, not the legislative convoke itself.

   The legislative must meet regularly but not permanently.

   The legislative can examine execution of executive but *cannot* question or judge his person; his counsellors may be both questioned and judged.

   The legislative's proper right is statutory, not limitative.

   It should enact money bills from year to year, not permanently, lest it lose its power to the executive.

   To protect against encroachment of executive, the legislative should raise army; members to be (1) wealthy propertied class, (2) year volunteers or (3) if of the rabble, then liable to demissioning by the legislative at all times.

   The nobility (higher chamber) should be hereditary, incapable of initiating money bills.

2. Executive power:

   Granted to permanent body(ies) since general will is involved.

   Possesses essentially the right of limitation.

   Should be vested in the monarch (leader) to facilitate rapid action.

Must convoke and adjourn legislative at all times.
May not be questioned (in his person) by the legislative; his counsellors may be questioned and judged.
Must not encroach on law-making right of the legislature; role is limitative, not statutory.
Should not raise armies but should control army once formed.
Should never initiate money bills.

3. Judicial power:
In many ways, a negative power—i.e., no power at all.
Must not be a permanent body since involved with individuals.
Its role neither statutory, nor limitative, but strictly one of judgment: to punish crimes and moderate differences between parties.

In general, says Montesquieu, most European monarchies combine legislative and executive powers in the prince with the judicial granted to his subjects; this, for Montesquieu (as it did for Locke) constitutes a "moderate" government. Heretofore, Montesquieu had assigned *moderation* as principle to aristocracy. Thus, this tripartite government (English, to Montesquieu's mind), for all its monarchic bias is *not* the former type of monarchy to which Montesquieu had assigned the principle of honor. Italian republics, thinks Montesquieu, tend to combine all three powers in the same source and thus these republics enjoy less liberty than a monarchy. However, there is a pronounced degree of loss of liberty between these republics and another form of government combining, of necessity, the three powers in one head; this is "frightful despotism"—example: Turkey.

Montesquieu concludes this key chapter with a frank, although indirect, admission that a government where the three powers are separated (i.e., England) must represent the highest point of liberty a constitution can grant. He is careful to add that he means no disrespect for other governments; an excess even of liberty (as compared to a moderation of it) is not always desirable, he says without much persuasion. Following a life-long interest and growing conviction, he discerns the source of such separated government in the Germanic tribes described by Tacitus—"This beautiful system . . . found in the forests." Yet, like Locke in a similar place in his discussion of the problem, he observes that all human institutions are subject to change and warns that this ideal government will perish when the legislative power allows itself to be corrupted by the executive. That he again had contemporary England in mind is borne out by typical English reaction in private letters to Montesquieu.[22] Whether or not the system he analyzed was, in effect, the actual English system has given rise to much discussion; in many ways and particularly at this juncture in his book, the answer to that problem is relatively unimportant. "It is not my place," he says, "to examine whether or not the English really enjoy that liberty today. Enough for me to say that it is established by their laws, and I look no further." In many ways, it was just the opposite that was true: i.e., the English came close to enjoying that liberty although it was not so clearly written in their laws.

Much depends, in one's general comprehension of Montesquieu's contribution to western thought, upon the answer elicited in a given reader to two basic problems suggested here. If Montesquieu in effect did *not* describe the actual English constitution —and he did not do so accurately—then either his conclusions as to balance of power are vitiated, or his whole exposition of separation of powers remains theoretical, not to say ideal. The second problem stems, in a sense, from the first. If Montesquieu believes he is analyzing in fact the English constitutional system, then what is so apparent in his discussion—i.e., the supremacy of monarchy over republic in assuring liberty—must color the application of his tripartite balance and open to question the commonplace that Montesquieu was an architect of reform and an apologist of the common man.

Montesquieu's analysis of the English system in Book XI must be completed by what he has to say touching on this system, later in *The Spirit* and later in time of composition (*ca.* 1746), in Book XIX, Chapter 27. That chapter ("How laws can contribute to the formation of customs, manners and character of a nation") is not clearly marked England, but it is a masterful study of English character. Once again, however, one is forced to ask whether we have not here a character sketch of a particular people rather than information on a particular kind of political liberty. Doubtless, in this chapter, Montesquieu's aim was the former; yet there are inevitable moments when he seems to be discussing more the free nation than the English nation.

Among many other things, he talks of political party, an important part of the English scene that he had completely ignored in the chapter on political liberty. The legislative and executive, naturally, encourage the formation of two power-pressure groups; particularly as the executive controls appointments and honors. Thus a basic parliamentary-tory party division. But Montesquieu had seen party action at first hand and particularly through the writings of Bolingbroke. There was a danger in oversimplifying a Whig-Tory split; there were in effect many colorations of both Whig and Tory just as there have always been realignments within any liberal-conservative tradition. These political passions are healthy and mark the healthy state; liberty dwells precisely in the continual changing of party. The executive, whatever his prestige abroad, will be "almost always harassed inside the state." "If the nobles had had during a certain time an immoderate power in the nation and the monarch had found the means of humbling them while elevating the people, the point of extreme servitude would have been between the moment of noble humiliation and that moment when the populace had begun to feel its power." The only danger is that the spirit of faction might encourage its partisans to take for truth the party line and thus "become as much slave to the prejudices of [one's] faction as to a despot." Montesquieu, in a very real sense, did not heed his own analysis here and took apparently for truth of the contemporary political scene (e.g., Bolingbroke's praise of separation of powers in *The Craftsman*)[23] what was policy dictated by heat of political faction. For, in effect, the English system did *not* show a clear tripartite separation of powers: e.g., the royal power over legislation had fallen into practical disuse; lords, as Montesquieu himself says, being legislative, still enjoyed certain judicial powers, etc.

On the score of the first problem then, I think one must say that Montesquieu, as always, was using England as his example *in history* and whether or not he thought he was describing it accurately is beside the point. In effect, such inaccuracy cannot vitiate his conclusions, for these conclusions, like the whole work, aim at analyzing the *spirit* of a particular institution. For Montesquieu, then, the *spirit* of a free government would remind one of the *actual* government of England. But his fixing of that spirit in optimum fashion in a government enjoying the separation of legislative, executive, and judicial powers, is his own ideal conclusion developed out of his empirical knowledge of England and his equally ideal theory of political liberty. After him, many nations will take his theory for authority; therein lies his genius and of this influence of Montesquieu on future generations more later. Robert Shackleton in the conclusion to his chapter on Liberty has summed up well, with his usual concern for accuracy, this whole problem: "The separation of powers, during Montesquieu's stay in England, was no more than a partisan cry. It was he who dignified and rationalized the concept, linked it to a theory of liberty; and handed it to posterity as a doctrine far more practical than its proponents had known." Yet it was clearly the English experience that crystallized his thinking. He thought it was based more or less on actuality (the English government) and he saw such a government working well toward the goal of political liberty. We are far removed here from the quasi-*a priori* generalizations of the first chapters. The separation of powers as Montesquieu stated it is an excellent example of the peculiar experimental scientific method that lies at the center of his life-long work.

The second problem—monarchy-republic—can now more readily be treated in the light of the above. Montesquieu's personal preference in governments is naturally and understandably for monarchy. One is not a baron (and a marquis)[24] for nothing. And yet he knew, whatever his protestations of fidelity and patriotism (and that patriotism was sincere), that France under the Regency and Louis XV, whatever the strength of its guiding principle *honor,* was far from achieving political liberty as he saw it. That England seemed to have achieved such a degree of liberty was not solely attributable to its being a monarchy, but the fact must not have saddened Montesquieu. In many of his commentaries on English government, it is true that the reader would find it hard to substitute the executive power of a republic or democracy like, for example, the United States. Yet Montesquieu does not make the monarch the sole possible executive; he is aware of many combinations for that seat of power. That he does seem to distrust the people—much as did Hamilton fifty years later—cannot be denied. But all of this does not invalidate the theoretical value of his separation ideal. Nor does it prevent us from seeing several aspects of his thinking that are, in terms of his period and position, liberal and reformist in spirit. Indeed his clearest warning to the partisans of political liberty is couched in pro-legislative, not pro-executive terms: "The [free] State will perish when the legislative power [of which part is nobility, to be sure] will be more corrupt than the executive."

VI *Philosophical Attitudes: Determinism and Pessimism*

Montesquieu's life spans the period in France that might be called the first movement, or preparation, of the Enlightenment. He knew some of the *philosophes* well (Helvétius, Jaucourt) and was accepted by some of them, at least, as one of their own. But the question as to whether he is, himself, to be considered a *philosophe* remains even in the twentieth century. One of the problems involved is to know precisely what a *philosophe* was and although this is not an idle question, it is one too complicated to enter upon here. If one requires of a *philosophe* that he be atheist and revolutionary, then Montesquieu was certainly not one, nor were many of the seminal writers we think of as the *philosophes*. If one's definition can be couched in such a way as to insist upon the paramount virtue of reason in man, of tolerance in one's view of God, and in a willingness to change man's future lot, then Montesquieu was eminently a *philosophe*.

It would be very wrong to suppose that Montesquieu was duplicitous in his attack against atheism. However great his admiration for Pierre Bayle (and he was attacked for it), he was simply incapable of accepting that Bayle's liberal attitude toward atheists could be part of an otherwise serious mind.[25] It would be wrong to suppose that Montesquieu was either anti-Christian or non-Christian. But it would be equally wrong to suppose that he was a noncritical Catholic or that he was imbued with the proselytist's conviction that Christianity was the only true religion. The works and particularly the personal notes of Montesquieu are eloquent as to his attitudes toward and critical strictures against aspects of the Catholic Church. He has little to say about the fact that his wife remained a Protestant and, indeed, sometimes suggests that Protestantism can in many ways encourage the *virtue* of which he speaks so often, better than Catholicism. But he remained a practicing Catholic to the end (France was Catholic and he was French) and it would be quite wrong to suppose that he harbored personal preferences for Protestantism. As in government, so in religion, the religion that conformed best to the character of a nation and was practiced with least difficulty and injustice was the best religion for that particular nation. This general conviction explains his open hatred for the Spanish conquest and Inquisition as well as the attacks made against him after publication of *The Spirit* for his less than orthodox views of Christian missions. There was no great benefit, he thought, to be derived from forcibly or even persuasively changing the religion of a given people.[26] Although certainly not so schematic as Voltaire on this score, Montesquieu nonetheless encourages an attitude toward religion that can only be called theistic, if not indeed, deistic. That Montesquieu believed in God, there can be no doubt; and that he attached to that belief the source and preservation of morality, but very little.[27] Just as God stood, so to speak, outside of the other natural laws, just so did God remain the fountainhead of all government. It was man's reason (God-given, of course) that eventually could and must discover for himself the truth of government, a purely human and social phenomenon. But this must not mean that, like Descartes' God viewed by Pascal, God was a completely impersonal force who, once having given physical impulse to Creation, withdrew completely.[28] He does not intervene at every moment into human affairs but he has endowed man with reason, and things with an ascertainable nature. The virtuous man and the reasonable man are, therefore, not virtuous and reasonable solely by their own efforts, but rather virtuous and reasonable in God, whether he be Catholic, Protestant, Christian, Moslem, or Hindu God. That is to say that, God being an indisputable and absolute fact, man's knowledge of him must remain relative.[29] But, reflecting the constant conviction of all of Montesquieu's works beginning with *The Persian Letters,* what is relative is not null, or negligible, or necessarily untrue.

This sense of the relative characterizes all of Montesquieu's philosophical outlook. That he was drawn to an idealistic interpretation of the world is inherent in his early admiration for Plato and, as we have seen, this desire for absolutes colors some of the first chapters of *The Spirit.* But his knowledge of the world as it was and his continuing curiosity to know more of it soon made such a metaphysical position difficult and scarcely consequent with the nature of things. Yet, in a curious way, Montesquieu continues to reflect a nostalgia for the absolute, and scholars have been justified in sensing an occasional duality in his method: now *a priori,* now empirical. Perhaps this duality may be clarified, if not explained away, by proposing that Montesquieu, like all good social scientists after him, stepped purposely out of his own occidental identity (the Persians had given him experience) to examine mores and manners in, as it were, a vacuum. For the average man, this shift into such an objective personality constitutes an excursion into an unaccustomed reality: one might say, the scientist's reality. But with Montesquieu the humanist is never lost or misplaced. Whatever the findings of that impersonal world of reality, Montesquieu must return to his own reality and his own skin and that meant a return to a French gentleman of the Catholic eighteenth century. The traditional beliefs had somehow to be harmonized with the novel ways of viewing human nature. From the facts Montesquieu (as the title assures us) insisted upon extracting a spirit; the facts were, of course, relative; but the spirit . . . , that, for Montesquieu, somehow had to possess qualities of universality. Thus the tones of duality so easy to discern in the general definitions of the first chapters when contrasted with the rest of the work.

This distinction between two frames of mind or two personalities in Montesquieu results in a parallel problem as concerns the application of the law: shall the law be applied in such a way as to encourage the improvement of a given civilization? The question is, of course, fraught with seeming confusions of terminology. For if, according to Montesquieu's central theory, laws derive from the nature of things: climate, customs, religion, governmental principle, and nature, etc. . . . , then they are determined naturally and they could no longer be so determined if they were liable to change and applicable to a better or different civilization than that by which they were produced. In other words, can one hold that laws are *caused* naturally, and then attempt to manipulate these effects so as to *cause* a set of circumstances no longer the same as those that had determined the laws initially? Upon the answer to this question hinges one's final estimate of Montesquieu's philosophical position and social contribution: whether or not he is a determinist; whether or not, a reformer; whether or not, a spokesman for "progress."

Expressed in simplest and not excessively superficial terms, a familiar burden of Montesquieu's truth might be: a particular government, a particular religion, a code of laws exist because they are the natural result of a peculiar set of circumstances (general spirit); the best government, religion, laws are those that conform most easily to the general spirit and operate with greatest ease. Thus one might suppose that a certain small Northern republic got the government it deserved; the large Slavic nation, the despotism it deserved; the island of moderate and phlegmatic character, the constitutional monarchy it deserved; a tropical people, the popular democracy or the tyrannical monarchy it deserved; etc. These things seem *fated* (a word Montesquieu, however, detests) to happen or determined by the nature of things and despite temporary "accidents." Montesquieu, in the *Romans* and throughout *The Spirit* is firm on this score; if Charles XII had not lost at Poltava, he would, necessarily, have been lost in the same way elsewhere; "if a chance battle [that is to say, a particular cause] has ruined a State, there was a general cause that operated in such a way that the State had to perish in a single battle." [30] The frame of mind here would seem already deterministic, to be sure, but in Montesquieu's, as in Diderot's notion of determinism, there is a supremely minor force of action granted to the human actor. If (and it is a large supposition) that actor—in this case, let us say the legislator—has understood well enough the nature of things that have produced the general spirit of his people, he may take a slight, although decisive, action to cancel one of those determinants by a gratuitous change of legislation. He will make such a free act advisedly, out of his knowledge of past experience with this people in this particular nature of things. Thus, he might possibly have discouraged the single battle of the sort (as Montesquieu says above) in which the nation was to perish, although all else would encourage his people to give battle. There is no other viable explanation for a work called the *Spirit of Laws* upon which our philosopher had spent a lifetime gleaning experience. At least the legislator will be spared a duplication of that scholarly research; he has before him a quintessence of law. Similarly, in other fields, other minds may have given corresponding quintessences. Not all the people, certainly, and not every legislator will be capable of using such quintessence to optimum ends; indeed, the handbook distilled from past experience can only be sometimes fallible. But within these narrow limits, the direction of the general spirit can be changed by law and thus encourage a new general spirit, generating new laws that presumably grant more liberty and more happiness. And Montesquieu can, in this fashion, be exonerated equally from grim fatalism and confusion of aims.

"Thus pure air is sometimes harmful to those who have lived in countries of swampy miasma." This is a key phrase of one of the most important books of *The Spirit*—Book XIX. Montesquieu's theme—"a very broad one," as he says—is, among other things, that for "better" laws, minds must be prepared. It is here, too, that he gives his clearest definition of the *general spirit*. But, above all, he tries to show that laws can contribute to customs and morals just as customs and morals, *et al.*, had contributed to the formation of laws. For Montesquieu, this was far from being a rhetorical paradox. Still, the reader is immediately aware of falling into, precisely, a paradox. Which comes first, the chicken or the egg? Which influences which—life, literature; or literature, life? It is of the nature of these timeless questions that Montesquieu's idea here partakes. Do laws form and encourage moral stamina; or are they but the inflexible reflection of prevailing morals? Montesquieu was certainly not a moralizer, but he was just as certainly a moralist. Although this fact is not perhaps obvious in his work to the superficial reader, to miss it is to miss the true significance of the *Spirit of Laws*. With the basic problem determinism-reformation in mind, one must say that Montesquieu's peculiar role as moralist was to realize, in this avant-garde period of the Enlightenment, that one could not create morality *a priori,* from revelation and/or the heart, but that what could be said about it needed to be realistically (and therefore, sometimes, pessimistically) grounded in a knowledge of human history and the nature of things. For if the Idea of morality had for Montesquieu its own peculiar sort of natural, not to say, absolute reality, the manifestations of it that could be known here below were strictly bound to man's body, mind, environment, and past conditioning.

It is all the more natural, therefore, to want to know something of Montesquieu's own preferences in this work that purported to be objective and scientific. Just as Montesquieu, the Catholic, seemed to prefer Catholicism,[31] personally, just so does Montesquieu, the French baron, seem to prefer French monarchy, personally. " . . . the democratic state is the liberty of the poor and weak and the servitude of the rich and powerful; and monarchy is the liberty of the great and the servitude of the little." [32] Such frank statements make believable other frequent confessions of faith—whatever the part of diplomacy and discretion to be assigned to them in the censored France of his day—such as: "I am a good citizen because I love the government under which I was born, without fearing it." However, he had already said, some lines before: "I am a good citizen, but in whatever country I might have been born, I should have still been one." The personal and the objective are allied here just as when he says: "The best of governments is ordinarily that under which one is living and a reasonable man ought to love it; for, as it is impossible to change government without changing manners and morals, I cannot conceive, given the extreme brevity of life, what use it would be for men to leave completely the rut they have made." [33] On one of several other occasions he points out that in France he is religious and eager for wealth in a certain way whereas he would be quite a different man in England. All of these limitations and relativities taken into account, however, it seems perfectly clear that Montesquieu prefers that government (republic or monarchy or aristocracy) that allows the maximum of liberty accompanied by morality in keeping with the potential of the citizens. The few pages he leaves us in his *Pensées* on the general subject of his notion of ideal institutions may help us to understand what may appear too general in the above approximation of his preference.[34]

Those pages are, however, extremely detailed and may suffer from an opposite excess. From the general to the specific, Montesquieu, centering his remarks on a favorite subject—inheritance laws, gives succinct recommendations: all males to inherit equally (at least, no one of them to enjoy more than a third more), females, in general, a third less than males. In a household, the husband shall control all money; in case of divorce, a division shall be made of one-third to wife, one-third to children and one-third to husband. He has little patience with bachelors and childless couples; parents of seven, six, and five children, on the other hand, enjoy varying benefits: it is true that Montesquieu worried about depopulation, not overpopulation. The morals of women are under the close surveillance of law. Firm suggestions are made for lawsuits and for ecclesiastical livings. In short, Montesquieu in these interesting notes, seems concerned with money and specific detail. Where, one might ask, is the spirit of the law? But these are but notes and we must not require too much of them. What we must see, I think, is that Montesquieu proposes to *change* legislation, at once with an eye to the natural familial nature of things, but also in the direction of what seems best to a French male who has given long consideration to the laws.

Thus it must be for Montesquieu in every province of human existence. We cannot choose a good of which we are ignorant. In the case of Montesquieu's ideal institutions touching upon inheritance, all will certainly not agree—not the Watusi or the Hopi, for their general spirit is not the Frenchman's. And probably not the twentieth-century Frenchman, for his historical moment (the age of rocket, television, and alienation) is no longer the same as that of an eighteenth-century gentleman. All is then relative? Yes, certainly as concerns human affairs. All is then gratuitous and fortuitous? No, not if men do not choose it to be so. All is then free and man can do exactly as he pleases and still find a modicum of happiness? No, for happiness must take into account the very physical relationships of man's corporal "machine" as well as the relationships (historical, climatic, etc.) of his social "machine." Only when he is aware of all the parts, and aims at best regulating the optimum play of these individual elements within the larger corpus (moderation in the body physical, moderation and mutual check-and-balance in the body politic), can he hope to see relative and absolute in proper perspective. "When it is said that there is no absolute quality, it doesn't mean there is none at all, but that there is none in us, and that our mind cannot resolve such qualities." [35] But our mind can, by a sustained and reasonable search into the nature of things, into the *spirit* of laws, approximate what is the rough dimension of the absolute, for that it *is* somewhere, Montesquieu never doubts. "We must clarify laws by history, and history by laws." The process, as we have seen, works both ways: custom creates law, law creates custom. But unlike Rousseau and the revolutionaries, the place to start (chicken-egg, egg-chicken again) is not by assuming that we must be free ("Man is born free, etc."), and by destroying the past to make political *tabula rasa*, but rather by conserving what has come down to us and by changing that within the limits of what we can know of political liberty by observation. In other words, men cannot know of something called liberty except by seeing how that commodity has manifested itself in the past; the absolute, Liberty, escapes us. It is conservative analysis that informs us on the varying degrees of liberty and suggests to us the best working of all political parts to produce the highest degree of liberty. The callow youth shouting liberty is mouthing a word, attempting to annex an idea about which he knows little. He sees it as a thing to be possessed with no outlay of intellectual energy but rather by brute force; he confuses liberty with license, and revolution (in Montesquieu's terms) with rebellion. A thorough conservative, not to say reactionary, this Montesquieu, the modern reader will say, as generations have said before him. The modern reader—for whom the words "conservative" and "liberal" have, unknown to him, lost all sense in the miasma of propagandistic exhalation—makes a grievous mistake; Montesquieu was a liberal.

What the modern occidental reader finds, naturally, very hard to achieve is the kind of objectivity that would permit him to retrace Montesquieu's intellectual experience. The average, presumably advised, Western citizen would find it just as unsettling to have questioned his unexamined prejudice for what he calls democracy as Montesquieu must have found it to question the universal validity of monarchy. As we have seen, he did not choose to question it personally. It was on the intellectual level that he began to see that a different sort of monarchy (constitutional) and eventually a non-monarchic republic or democracy—given proper balance—could guarantee, as it had at rare moments guaranteed, a larger measure of political liberty. Of course, to the average man of 1740, monarchy seemed natural and predestined and the apologies of all the Bossuets could only confirm the comfortable prejudice of the Versailles commuter that he lived in the best of all possible worlds. It is in that light that one must see Montesquieu's continued search for truth in a nation where censorship discouraged such search. Naturally, the have-nots (as has always been the case: in Rome, for example) were not happy with that best of all possible worlds. They were incapable of reading and understanding *The Spirit;* they were not yet to be whipped into action in the name of a liberty they understood badly. As for most men, when action came, it was much easier to direct it toward sweeping clean rather than patching up. It has always seemed easier to blow up a bridge rather than study painfully how best to place bracing to alleviate faulty stress and strain; much simpler to demolish the house rather than undergo the slow process of staying up or changing faulty foundations. Montesquieu's way was the way of careful study before action.

Other temperaments prefer other ways. But history has borne out Montesquieu, at least in part: we cannot change until we know as thoroughly as possible what and how to change. That he preferred a minimum of change lays him open to charges of conservatism. That he dared to suggest the value of change in a world of relativity, when all about him encouraged his complacency, marks him as a liberal of 1750. When we understand the interplay of "patching-up" and ideal check-and-balance equilibrium seen as early as the Troglodytes, he becomes a liberal for all time.

The source of his warm desire for amelioration, for reform, is to be found in Montesquieu's humanism more readily than in his political science. No doubt, he would have been happy to know for sure that he had removed all personal meditation and aspiration from his scientific work; the simple fact is that he was incapable of it, for the whole man intrudes, happily, at every moment in his work. He is not, after all, our idea of a professional philosopher; like Thoreau and Montaigne, he philosophizes on his readings and his life. He borrows from many, can be called a disciple of none of his celebrated predecessors. In Hobbes, he cannot accept the basic premise of human bellicosity, however tempting many times; Spinoza's system is suspect for its impersonal God; Locke is almost too exclusively the apologist of law as property-protection; Bayle, too close to rank materialism and atheism. No system could adequately clothe what he had to say about the spirit of laws for, if there was, in fact, an ideal Spirit in the Platonic spheres, there were equally, in fact, sets of determining circumstances that, like everything human, changed continually. Even as concerns his country of predilection, England, the English themselves soon understood the subtle conditions he placed on his glorification of that island. An Englishman, Domville, wrote to Montesquieu: "You feel more what we are than what we *ought* to be, that our liberty has turned to license, that the very idea of the common weal is lost and that the fate of rich and corrupted nations awaits us, even that we are rushing on toward that corruption." [36]

Montesquieu, happy in his personal life, in his family life, in his social life, Montesquieu who was once drawn to write: "Happiness or unhappiness consists in a certain disposition, favorable or unfavorable, of our organs";[37] this same Montesquieu was engaged in the future, and ways in which the future could be brighter. Certainly, in many carefully couched remarks, he makes suggestions as to reforms to be carried out in France, as he does occasionally for England and other European countries. His thinking is in a true sense cosmopolitan and one senses that it is with regret that he says that international law has, as yet, no distinct character or principle. Which does not mean that it will never have such principle. Personal happiness may indeed be a question of physical organs; national happiness consists in an eternal return to first principles—whether the nation be monarchy or republican, and international happiness must consist in the searching out of a new international principle liberally based on personal and national experience. What he did write, as we have seen, is a varied collection of character sketches or psychological studies *and* a digest of national traits and social organization. What he did not touch upon were the bases of a true world government, but his view of the future envisaged it. The human psyche could not be totally remade, nor could the facts about social organization in historical times be ignored. But somehow, if his theories were valid, laws could manage to influence customs for the better (more liberty for more people) just as past customs had influenced the formation of present laws.

For Montesquieu, as for most of the *philosophes* after him, however, the process of change was preferably and perhaps necessarily a slow one. Like Diderot after him, he fears the effect of hasty action on the prestige of law in general. "For this reason, one ought not to make laws on unimportant issues: for the man who breaks a useless law will diminish respect for those necessary to Society; and, so soon as he has broken faith by violating one point, he will follow his own convenience by violating all the others that inconvenience him." [38] There are, of course, bad laws, laws that should never have been passed and that stand sometimes an eternity on statute books because the legislator has forgotten one of Montesquieu's most succinct statements of the spirit of law. "A thing is not just," he writes in his *Pensées*, "because it is law; but it should become law because it is just." [39] Bad laws are, therefore, a violation of the whole concept of liberty, but liberty may probably be lost more quickly by frenzied change of laws than by the existence of unjust laws. For Montesquieu, change in itself was no virtue and novelty almost always led to greater injustice. Shackleton sees a direct influence of Bolingbroke on Montesquieu here—the Bolingbroke who had written in *The Craftsman:* ". . . in the greatest revolution [Cromwell's] of the greatest government [England] of the world, losing the spirit of liberty was the cause and losing liberty was the effect." [40] Losing the spirit of the laws—ignoring the *esprit général* and other elements in legislating—could patently lead to the same effects: loss of liberty. And losing an advised sense of relativity—whether in making or unmaking laws—was the quickest way to lose the creative and conserving power of law. Reason is our only guide, to be sure ("Laws are human reason"), but reason must not be taken to mean the pure empyrean reason of Plato, rather the practical reason of common-sense observation. Like Descartes, Montesquieu takes firm exception to Bayle (already attacked for his supposed atheism) on this score: "It was stupid of Bayle to say that a republic of good Christians could not endure; and that's because there could not be a republic of good Christians. Just so, when we say that a republic of philosophers could not endure, the whole point is that there could not be a republic of philosophers. All is mixed together." [41]

Thus the laws and the changing of them must be gauged specifically, an individual case for each nation. England, for example, does not derive equal influence from *all* the elements contributing to the *esprit général,* as a notation in the *Pensées* makes clear: "The English nation has scarcely any manners, nor even any customs peculiar to that nation. At best, she possesses an enlightened respect for Religion. She is profoundly attached to her own particular laws; and these laws must have a tremendous influence when they defy or favor the climate." [42] The particular situation of England, much as Montesquieu admired it, made it paramount that laws (in her case, according to him, a foremost determinant of laws) be preserved in so far as possible, and Montesquieu makes clear that, in her case, the loss of liberty (i.e., the corruption of government) will come from a betrayal of the legislative to the executive.

In a moment, no doubt, of relaxation, Montesquieu exercises his wit in a notation, never, of course, to appear in print. It is amusing and informative. "I was saying: 'What an extraordinary thing that all philosophy should consist in these [in French] three words: I don't give a damn.' " [43] The reader is confused, I believe, only for a moment, but he is confused. For, after all, Montesquieu did give a damn, did glorify human reason, and did spend a lifetime of deep concern for that most superb of human achievements, the law. The proper reading of the note is, I believe, simply this, and it provides a fine conclusion to any discussion of Montesquieu, the philosopher. Truth must be sought without prejudice, without prior commitment, as if one did not give a damn. The Baron de Montesquieu had his personal preferences: for the nobility, for the monarchy, for landed estates, for marriage of convenience, for male supremacy, etc. But the conclusions reached after the long study of all the laws history can inform us about, must be severed from all personal preference. There is perhaps no finer statement in all of his writing than this much quoted passage from the *Pensées* reflecting the graceful and admirable marriage within Montesquieu of the humanist and philosopher. Montesquieu was so fond of the passage that he composed it in several forms; it stands as his philosophical emblem. "If I knew something useful to me and harmful to my family, I should put it out of my mind. If I knew something useful to my family and not to my country, I should try to forget it. If I knew something useful to my country and harmful to Europe, or useful to Europe and harmful to the human race, I should consider it a crime." [44] As the *Spirit of Laws* seems to point continually in the direction of international law as being man's eventual summit short of God's absolute law, just so does Montesquieu's intellectual and emotional experience lead him toward true cosmopolitism. "You are a good Frenchman and a good Cosmopolite," writes the Protestant pastor, Vernet, from Geneva after the *Spirit*. That cosmopolitism is one of the enduring hallmarks of the French Enlightenment. Here, certainly, Montesquieu set the tone for the whole century.

CHAPTER 4

Literary Fortunes

> . . . *je ne demande autre chose à la terre que de continuer à tourner sur son centre.*[1]

THE *Spirit of Laws* evoked, as we have seen, an immediate reaction upon its publication in 1748. Cries of "genius" were mixed with cries of "inaccurate" and "unwholesome," and Montesquieu went to his grave certainly a little confused by the reluctance of men of good will to try to understand what he had spent twenty years doing. His death did not silence criticism and reaction; his name and reputation were firmly established then, and remain so now. He has never needed to be "rediscovered."

It is possible and helpful, I think, to discuss his literary fortunes under three heads: reaction in France during the age of Enlightenment; reaction abroad during the same general period, particularly in England and America; and his more general acceptance by the world in general, particularly the social scientists, from the nineteenth century on.

I *Montesquieu and the Enlightenment*

The critical reaction immediately after the publication of *The Spirit*, as we have seen, was vociferous and varied. Even if we discount the obviously factious attacks, it is clear that many scholars found many points of serious contention with both the aim and the methods of the generally admired *président*. But a discussion of those critics—names for the most part unknown to posterity—interests us not so much here as a hopefully more fertile discussion of the reactions of the important representatives of the philosophic movement.

II *Montesquieu and Helvétius*

Helvétius, intimate friend of Montesquieu and admirer of his character and intellect, was far from happy with the work. This *fermier général*,[2] devoted to the battle of enlightenment, who was later to add to it two important titles—*On the Mind* (1758) and *On Man* (posthumous, 1770)—would have preferred that the book never appear; in any case, it should have been thoroughly revised before appearing. Himself imbued with a materialism only slightly less severe than that of La Mettrie, he discusses his apprehensions in a letter to his friend. He is, first of all, wary of Montesquieu's idealism:

> . . . but you too often give the world credit for reason and wisdom, which are in fact your own, and with which it will be much surprised to be honored.[3]

This limitation placed on the efficacy of reason by a *philosophe* should not surprise, for, contrary to an all-too-current judgment of the Enlightenment as naïve, most of the *philosophes* were aware of the gradual nature of the process. In almost the next breath, however, Helvétius takes Montesquieu to task for, precisely, not putting sufficient stress on what the laws *ought* to be and not demanding immediate action toward changing them. This was to be a general disillusionment of the *philosophes* who assumed Montesquieu was writing a different kind of book about the laws. "But," writes Helvétius:

> I concluded that a writer, anxious to serve mankind, ought to lay down just maxims for an improved order of things yet to arise, rather than to give force or consequence to those which are dangerous, at the moment when prejudice is striving to preserve and perpetuate human ignorance and subjection. To employ philosophy in giving them consequence is to give human genius a retrograde motion. . . .[4]

On specific points, Helvétius thinks that what has turned out to be Montesquieu's single most important contribution to future thinking, the separation of powers, "only tend[s] to separate and complicate individual interests, rather than to unite them." Not as clear as other critics on Montesquieu's partial comprehension of the English government, Helvétius says only: "The example of the English government has seduced you." Naturally (or perhaps not so naturally coming from a *fermier général*), Helvétius can scarcely understand the all-important role granted by Montesquieu to the "intermediaries" of Versailles: the priests and the nobles. Helvétius misses the whole point of what he calls Montesquieu's "subtleties": the discussion of governments by nature and principle, the force of the "*esprit général,*" etc. There are simply good governments and bad governments, says Helvétius, and only the diffusion of knowledge will make good government possible; "I dare to predict that we approach such an epoch." In a letter to Saurin, Helvétius touches on that sore point for many of Montesquieu's critics: the last books on the question of Frankish influence of feudal law. He wonders aloud to Saurin "what the devil" Montesquieu would have us understand by these extraneous books. He suspects the worst (mistakenly, of course) and sees in those final books an apology for, rather than an explanation of, feudalism. "Ought we then," he asks Saurin, "to inherit all the errors that have been accumulating since the origin of the human race?" [5]

III *Montesquieu and Condorcet*

Diderot, the only *philosophe,* we are told, to be present at Montesquieu's funeral, says singularly little about him; one suspects he came closest to understanding the tremendous dimensions of Montesquieu's project and that his natural respect for the older *président* attenuates his reaction to possible points of disagreement. Condorcet, that Benjamin of the group and, so pathetically, its final spokesman, has left us pertinent remarks on the very important Book XXIX, "How Laws are made." For Condorcet, the true spirit of the legislator can be only justice; thus, understanding Montesquieu in spirit if not in letter, he is not satisfied with Montesquieu's continued insistence (particularly in discussing aspects of republics) upon the key word *moderation.*

> By the spirit of moderation, does not Monsieur Montesquieu understand that spirit of uncertainty which alters by a hundred irrelative motives, the principles of justice, which are in themselves invariable? [6]

In general, Condorcet, like Helvétius, is unimpressed by most of Montesquieu's efforts to categorize, analyze, and apply shadings to his various political groups. The vocabulary is many times inaccurate and uncertain, he says, and the over-all organization confused. Justice is justice, he insists, however described and "a good law should be good for all men." Thus Condorcet seems to refute the very heart of Montesquieu's thesis: that law and justice are relative to several interacting determinants. Again like Helvétius, he regrets Montesquieu's lethargy before the need for change:

> Repugnance to change can be reasonable only in these two cases: (1) When the laws of a country approach so near to reason and justice and the abuses are so trifling that no sensible advantage could be expected. (2) When it is supposed that there is no certain principle by which we might direct ourselves in security to the establishment of new laws. . . . Montesquieu looked upon legislation as a game, in which it is indifferent whether this or that path be followed, so that the established constitution, whatever it may be, is adhered to. But this is not true, even of gaming, where the rules, though apparently arbitrary, are almost all founded on reasons which the gamesters indistinctly perceive, and which mathematicians accustomed to the calculations of probabilities, can explain.[7]

Like so many of Montesquieu's critics, Condorcet is disappointed not to find specific suggestions (rather than analyses of past solutions) as to the process of legislation—*all* legislation. Having given some of his own ideas, he concludes that his ideas only scratch the surface and do not exhaust "the number of principles which should enter into the composition of a work on the manner of instituting laws." However necessary these principles are, he concludes, "Montesquieu has not thought it worth his while to employ his time upon them."

IV *Montesquieu and Rousseau*

Certainly the *philosophe* (one should better say *ex-philosophe* or *anti-philosophe*) who invites immediately our attention—if not to a lengthy commentary on Montesquieu, then to the seminal work that replies to and continues Montesquieu—is Jean-Jacques Rousseau. Particularly, the Rousseau of the first two discourses and, of course, the *Social Contract.* The name of Montesquieu appears only very rarely (once in the *Contract,* once in *Considerations on . . . Poland*) in Rousseau's political works, but Rousseau owes much to him if only because Montesquieu offers a sounding board against which to try his own ideas, a recently discussed model to serve him as partial pattern. Rousseau, as is his usual habit, quotes much more readily Grotius, Hobbes, and the Greek and Roman classics as being the more accepted authorities, but the *Spirit of Laws* is ever present to his mind as he works on the projected larger work that is eventually to become reduced to the *Social Contract,* published some five years after Montesquieu's death.

Like Montesquieu, Rousseau is unconcerned with discovering the true historic state of pre-social man; it is a hypothetical basis to relevant political theory. Like Montesquieu, Rousseau cannot accept Hobbes' dour description of that moment as a state of war. Thereafter, and running like a *leitmotiv* throughout all of Rousseau's thought, there is a significant difference between him and Montesquieu. However concerned, eventually, with the individual, Montesquieu might be described as the theorist of the State purveying justice to the individual. Rousseau's position seems completely reversed: the individual is the sole reality in search of a State, indeed dissolving into the State that preserves his individuality, however collective that individuality has grown. Yet, strangely enough, both men invoke that fugitive commodity, reason. If Montesquieu states so pithily: "Law is human reason," Rousseau can resound in the same sense: "The body politic is but a being of reason." There is, of course, reason and reason.

From similar discussion of natural law, the two diverge as to basic notions of society and of society's creation, law. For Montesquieu, as we have seen, all effort was turned toward seeing law, however relative in detail, as a completely natural phenomenon; thus, with difficulty and somewhat idealistically, Montesquieu progresses, naturally, from the absolute of Natural Law to the relative of positive law. For Rousseau, society is an essentially artificial entity since man had no natural need of it and since there are no social bodies amongst natural bodies; thus Rousseau, too, must reconcile two conceptions: society as reason and society as an extra organism (something like Hobbes' Leviathan). On two points, similarity of language may help to distinguish Montesquieu and Jean-Jacques. If for Montesquieu, laws are relationships that derive from the nature of things, for Rousseau they are principles of society that "derive from the nature of things and are founded on reason." Very slight difference one might say, laws and principles of society, yet the use of language is revelatory as to basic prime concerns of the two men. We have seen in what sense Montesquieu uses his term *general spirit* to sum up all the interacting and relative determinants of law. When we fall upon Rousseau's *general will,* we see clearly that the term suggests not that which *has* determined the law, but rather that which remains to be achieved in order to conciliate the individual and society and thus to legislate justly. Montesquieu's term describes what was the fact and cause; Rousseau's searches for what must come about ideally to make laws possible. As he says in the *Emile,* we must put into law "a real force, superior to the action of all particular will," and find a form of government that puts law above man. Montesquieu, speaking to the same point, might more readily have said, we must find how the law came to be, so as continually to reintegrate man into it.

What each has to say on liberty is equally revealing. For Montesquieu, liberty in a State (i.e., a society where there are laws) "can consist only in being able to do what one ought to want to do and not to be forced to do what one ought not to want." Rousseau's definition, superficially, is strikingly similar: "Liberty consists less in doing one's will than in not being subjected to the will of another, it consists also in not subjecting another's will to ours. Whoever is master cannot be free." The point of view is again revelatory: Montesquieu's historical, Rousseau's merely conjectural, even if more dynamic. For both men, of course, the vital role in the achievement and conservation of liberty is the legislator's. Montesquieu's legislator, empirically formed, is the scholar and historian who can apply his experience to the role of changing the law in the good direction. Rousseau's legislator, in that almost mystic lighting that has confounded many a reader, is at once the legislator and the people. His laws reflect the general will and unite the universality of the will to the universality of the object. Montesquieu's legislator, when a bad one, could produce bad laws that sinned by ignoring the spirit of laws. Rousseau's legislator (if he becomes one at all) can never be unjust, for in legislating for the people he legislates for himself and "nobody can be unjust to himself."

In categorizing the laws (natural law aside), Montesquieu had distinguished as positive laws: international, political, and civil law. Rousseau speaks little of international law and identifies the other positive laws as: political (relationship between citizenry as sovereign and citizenry as subject), civil, and penal laws, and adds another. These last laws are customs, manners, opinions, etc. In other words, what Montesquieu had seen as a prerequisite determinant of law (his "*esprit général*"), becomes for Rousseau a law itself and not the least important, for these things form a society.

In short, Montesquieu's legislator must naturally be guided by the experience of things past, must, insofar as possible, measure positive law against natural law. For Rousseau, since all law is artificial, no one will can perform such a task ("we need gods to give laws to men") for the total citizenry *is* the legislator. Thus the general will—unlike Hobbes' strong executive, permanent since the social contract—does not seek to force obedience; it *is* obedience and justice since it is the all, and aims to form the citizenry so that resistance to law is a contradiction and obedience to law part and parcel of the law. There is little doubt that Rousseau's influence will be greater in the last part of the century and, indeed, ever since; his is a mystique of law rather than an analysis of its spirit. Yet, the French Revolution will seem many times to hesitate between these two theorists and follows now one, now the other. In general, conservative movements will call upon Montesquieu, more radical movements upon Rousseau. The very introductory paragraphs of their great works, *The Spirit* and the *Contract*, inform us about their different intentions. Montesquieu says there: "I first examined men and believed that, in that infinite diversity of laws and customs, they were not led solely by their fantasy." Rousseau, more succinctly, opens his work with the following sentence: "I wish to find out if, in the civil order, there can be some sure and legitimate rule of administration, taking men as they are, and laws as they can be." Montesquieu the psychologist and historian; Rousseau, the psychologist and reformer. Rousseau, in the second chapter of his work, in a footnote on Grotius quotes from a work of d'Argenson as follows: "The learned researches on public law are often but the history of ancient abuses; and scholars have persisted erroneously when they took pains to study them too much." "That," adds Rousseau, "is exactly what Grotius did." One senses that Rousseau might very well have liked to substitute for Grotius the name of Montesquieu.

V *Montesquieu and Voltaire*

One could scarcely speak of the opinion of the Enlightenment without consulting Voltaire. Understanding Voltaire's true impression of Montesquieu is not easy. That he admired the *président*, there can be no doubt; that he found him often pedantic, inaccurate, and ineffectual (in Voltaire's terms) is made sufficiently clear by the many references to Montesquieu in Voltaire's works. Voltaire's remarks on Montesquieu are particularly concentrated in two short works: a philosophic dialogue of the so-called *ABC* "On Hobbes, Grotius and Montesquieu" (in which Montesquieu receives most of Voltaire's attention), and the much longer work *Commentary on some important Maxims of the "Spirit of Laws"* (1777).[8] It would be impossible to do justice to all of Voltaire's commentary in a short space; he has, himself, limited his discussion to non-disputable points and not to those propositions "that one can attack and defend at length without agreeing on anything."

Voltaire's ciriticism, in general, is concentrated upon two aspects of *The Spirit,* certainly not immune from criticism before him. He does not understand the peculiar orientation of Montesquieu's mind that produces what passes for organization of his material. And he is shocked by the many gross inexactitudes and frequent downright errors left in the finished work. On the score of organization, Voltaire reflects perhaps the reaction of many readers: "I cannot keep from laughing as I leaf through more than a hundred chapters of only twelve lines each, and there are some that contain only two. It would appear that the author wanted to play continually with his reader on the gravest of material." As for the errors, they are legion and Voltaire takes perhaps more pleasure than he ought in quoting chapter and verse to correct them.

Aside from these general criticisms, the burden of Voltaire's comments, recurring on almost every page, echoes a common judgment of the century, originally attributable to the *salonnière* Mme du Deffand: that the Spirit (*esprit*) of Laws is too often only wit (*esprit*) about laws.[9] It is, at once, the manner and the method of Montesquieu that Voltaire criticizes under this blanket accusation of "too witty." Stylistically, Montesquieu is too often led for purposes of effect, into doubtful simile and comparison, as, for example when he writes: "Just as the sea, which seems to want to cover the earth, is stopped by the grasses and the smallest pebbles of the shore; thus monarchs, whose power seems limitless, are stopped by the smallest obstacle. . . ." Voltaire comments: "This is not the style of a legislator. But certainly it is neither the grass nor the pebble that causes the sea to recede, it is the law of gravity. . . ." Much more serious than lapses in taste,

Montesquieu's style leads him into a method that smells of dilettantism. Montesquieu introduces too many times into his discussion piquant anecdotes, now from this traveler in Japan, now from another in Borneo. Voltaire accuses Montesquieu of using any "authority" with equal trust, many times inaccurately and often with no relevancy to his subject, only to amuse his reader. "One should not talk so much," quips Voltaire, "of Indian and Japanese laws and customs which we know so badly, when there is so much to be said on our own which we ought to know." Thus, added to the charge of faulty method, there is joined here the by now familiar regret of all the *philosophes,* that Montesquieu did not choose (did not dare) to speak openly enough of the abuses at home.

Voltaire singles out many propositions for longer criticism, either on the score of inconsistent reasoning or of inaccurate documentation. Leaving aside (as was his pretended wont) all discussion of things metaphysical: natural law, pre-social man, etc. he centers his attention on propositions calculated to raise the hackles of this indefatigable pamphleteer. A typical (and succinct) commentary follows. Montesquieu had said: "The English, to promote liberty, have removed all the intermediary powers that formed their monarchy." Voltaire replies: "On the contrary, the English have made the power of spiritual and temporal lords more legal, and have enlarged the power of Commons. One is astonished that our author should have fallen into such an evident misunderstanding." Voltaire has ambiguous feelings generally toward Montesquieu's treatment of his favored nobility; the nobility is not so important as Montesquieu believes even in an "honor" monarchy, but this is no reason to describe it as Montesquieu occasionally does. Says Montesquieu: "It is not enough that there should be intermediate ranks [nobility] in a monarchy; we must also have a depository of laws. . . .the natural ignorance of the nobility, its unconcern and scorn for civil government, make necessary a body constituted to bring old laws out of the dust where they would be buried. . . ." Voltaire, shocked, writes a long and convincing rebuttal, then adds a pithy note: "Moreover, how can it be useful to a country that a body of men, ignorant, frivolous, filled with scorn for civil government, should be elevated above the citizens?"

Voltaire's attitude toward Montesquieu is that of the *magister,* filled with admiration for the potential of his disciple but disillusioned by his final efforts. "All these misapprehensions of the author of the *Spirit of Laws* make one regret that a book that could be so useful was not composed with proper care, and that the author almost always sacrifices truth to what is called wit." "When such a fine mind as Montesquieu errs, I am caught in other errors by uncovering his. This is the fate of all those who pursue truth. . . . I respect Montesquieu even when he falters, because he rises again to ascend to the very sky." We can perhaps best sum up his attitude by quoting a generalization from the *ABC* dialogue: "Montesquieu has much imagination on a subject that would appear to require only judgment. . . .Grotius is a fine pedant, Hobbes a sad philosopher and Montesquieu a human wit." If Voltaire seems sometimes unfair to Montesquieu, we must, on the other hand, not be too hasty in judging Voltaire. As so often in his life, he is really taking Montesquieu to task for not having written the book that he, Voltaire, would have written or have liked to see written on legislation. Like so many others, the true sense of Montesquieu's title and life-work escaped him.

VI *Montesquieu and the Revolution*

The French Revolution is, like all revolutions, an end and a beginning: an end to what is properly called the Enlightenment, the beginning of the brave new world of applied philosophy. One need not argue the point as to whether it, in effect, carried out the programs of Montesquieu, Voltaire, Diderot, Rousseau, *et al.* Diderot's influence on the Revolution is almost nil, Voltaire's very slight. The philosophic names perhaps most invoked by the writers of the Revolution are Montesquieu and Rousseau, with the latter by far in first place. In general, Montesquieu is the patron saint of the first half or constitutional era of the French Revolution, Rousseau consistently a guiding spirit, particularly in the movements to the extreme left. A representative mind of the period can be found in Saint-Just. His *Spirit of the Revolution* owes something to both Montesquieu and Rousseau, with certainly more personal warmth for the latter: "France has just, finally, voted a statue to Jean-Jacques Rousseau. Ah! why did that great man die?"

The original edition of the *Spirit of the Revolution* (1791), at the high moment of the Constituent Assembly, carried as epigraph a well-known quotation from Montesquieu: "If I could bring it about that everyone had new reasons to love his duties, his prince, his country, his laws and that he could better sense his happiness, I should think myself the happiest of mortals." The work, in a strange fashion, as if reflecting the pressures of the times, tries to conciliate or unite the ideas of Montesquieu and Rousseau; out of this ideologic fusion will grow the Jacobin political tradition that will triumph until the fall of both Robespierre and St.-Just in 1794. Thus St.-Just will talk at one and the same time of the various kinds of power, reminiscent of Montesquieu's separation theory and also of the sovereign in Rousseau's terms who is, at once, citizenry and ruler—executive, legislative, and judicial in one. In the early chapters of St.-Just's study where he attempts to describe the French Constitution (1791), his language recalls that of Montesquieu: a chapter is headed "Du rapport, de la nature et des principes de la Constitution," and successive passages spell out what is the nature and principle, *not* of forms of government as with Montesquieu, but of liberty, equality, and justice—already a blending as it were of Montesquieu and Jean-Jacques. For St.-Just has little reason to discuss forms of government (although surely aware of past commentary on them) since, as he tells us: "France [is] a united democracy, aristocracy, monarchy; the first forms the civil state, the second the legislative power and the third the executive power." He continues in the same place (Chapter I) in language echoing Montesquieu:

> When a people, become free, has established wise laws, its revolution is made; if these laws are in keeping with the territory, the revolution will endure. . . . Where there is perfect democracy (which is exaggerated liberty), no monarchy; where there is only aristocracy, no lasting laws; where a prince would be what he was formerly, no liberty. The powers had to be so modified that neither people, legislative body nor monarch could claim a tyrannical ascendency.

This concern for the balance of power elements echoes Montesquieu, as does his insistence in Chapter II on the individual over the state. He draws there a repeated contrast between ancient states where fatherland came first and the new France where "the rights of men are affirmed" and where "the fatherland forgets its own interests for those of its children." Yet almost immediately thereafter and to the end of his essay he continues speaking in terms of Rousseau's sovereign, where "fatherland" and "children" are fused into the single *volonté générale,* or general will, and this despite his continuing interest in class separation. "It has been said that where powers are not separated, there would be no constitution; it might have been added that where men would be socially equal, there could be no harmony." It is entrenched privilege, as opposed to natural and dynamic class distinction, that he attacks: "The nobility and the clergy . . . the rampart of tyranny, have disappeared with it; the first no longer exists and the second is now only what it should be." In this early movement of the revolution—"nation, king and law," the king marks an imporant power division, but he no longer *reigns,* he *governs:* "democracy makes the constitution, aristocracy makes the laws and the monarch governs!" "In France, the constitution is liberty, equality, justice; public spirit is sovereignty, fraternity, security; opinion is nation, law and king." It is easy to see how St.-Just had adopted Montesquieu's and Rousseau's terms to his own ends, however confusing they may be at times; it is also clear that he has attempted to keep them both, just as at this point of the Revolution he combines bourgeois reform with the seeds of Jacobinism. In an emotional outcry, we hear Montesquieu's axiom of return to principle coupled with Jean-Jacques' brand of virtue: "Oh Liberty, sacred liberty! You would be insignificant among men, if you made them only happy, but you recall them to their origins [cf. Montesquieu's principle] and you restore them to virtue." That he has still some misgivings (or rather, understands imperfectly Rousseau) is clear from a significant paragraph of his conclusion:

People will ask whether I believe seriously that the Constitution of France, such as it stands now, is the will of all [note that he does not use Rousseau's general will]: I reply categorically no; because it is impossible, when a people accepts a new contract (the first being lost or soiled) that rascals and malcontents not form two parties; but it would be a strange abuse of the letter to take the resistance of a few rascals for a part of the will. General rule: all will, even sovereign, that inclines toward perversity is null and void; Rousseau did not say everything when he characterized will as uncommunicable, non-prescriptible, eternal. It must also be just and reasonable.

St.-Just has not yet understood the true mystique of Rousseau's general will; he has not yet forgotten the traditional powers of Montesquieu's *Spirit*.

VII *Montesquieu and Destutt de Tracy*

Destutt de Tracy (1754–1836), child of the Enlightenment, chief of the ideologues, with his roots in the eighteenth century and his mature years in the nineteenth century, is an excellent spokesman for the transition mind that could view the Revolution and Napoleon in historical perspective. He has left us perhaps the first objective commentary on Montesquieu's *Spirit*, one that still qualifies as an important appraisal of Montesquieu's contribution to Western thought. When he finally published it in 1819, he wrote the following prefatory note, of particular interest to Americans. "This work has existed for over twelve years. I wrote it for Mr. Jefferson, the man of two worlds that I most respect, and if he were to judge it appropriate, for the United States of North America where it was indeed printed in 1811. I did not plan to publish it in Europe. But since an inexact copy was current there, printed at Liège and then at Paris, since everyone is printing my work without my permission, I prefer to have it appear as I wrote it." Destutt's commentary appeared first in English, along with Condorcet's remarks on Montesquieu's Book XXIX and two letters of Helvétius touching on Montesquieu's work.[10]

In his preliminary remarks, Destutt de Tracy, using the term social science in referring to Montesquieu, promises to be as frank and objective as he can and not to let himself be overly impressed by the reputation and fame of a great man. He carries out this promise immediately, falling upon Montesquieu's famous definition of law: "A law," he objects, "is not a relationship, and a relationship is not a law." Montesquieu's explanation lacks clear meaning. He does understand the true meaning of Montesquieu's title: "The spirit of laws, that is to say, the spirit in which laws are or ought to be made." But like others, he is put off by the formal organization of the work. The first twelve books contain all that is directly concerned with the organization of society and the distribution of its powers; thereafter, there are spotty *hors d'oeuvre*. In particular the last books (XXVII, XXVIII, XXXI) "have but very remote connection with the subject that occupies them." Like many another son of the Enlightenment he would have liked Montesquieu to show a closer connection between reason and nature. He affirms that the principle of governments founded on the rights of man is Reason but he shows that "governments founded upon reason need only to let Nature work and follow her without opposing her." He is particularly interested in Montesquieu's discussion of liberty and on several occasions attempts to clarify Montesquieu's text with his own notions on the subject. Man being an atom in the immensity of beings, is endowed with sensitivity (this, from Condillac) and, then, with will. His happiness consists in accomplishing this will for which execution he has very little power. But such power as he has *is* liberty. "Let us conclude," he says, "that liberty comes only after will and in relation to it and that liberty is but the power of executing the will." His own prescription for a reasonable government, cutting through Montesquieu's more formal descriptions and analyses of forms of government, can be simply given: (1) it should be a government of the governed, (2) it should never found such a power as cannot be changed non-violently, (3) its goal should be to preserve independence of the citizen.

His commentary on Montesquieu's Book XXVI—so important to *The Spirit* as to constitute a kind of conclusion to the work on the proper application of specific laws to specific cases—is so short and so representative of his critical style that it is, perhaps, helpful to reproduce it here in its entirety. One suspects he did not quite grasp Montesquieu's intention, nor consider the 1748 work from an historical point of view, yet he does cut through some of Montesquieu's hesitation and verbiage.

Under a title sufficiently enigmatical, all this book can be reduced to a single point; that we should not decide on a question by the same motives which induced the determination of another question of quite a different nature. This is too evident for anyone to attempt to deny it. I shall not occupy myself therewith, inasmuch as all decisions on numerous objects, which are made upon the authority of precedents or examples, are in fact prejudgments; or judgments given upon evidence that has nothing to do with the subject: at least this is my manner of seeing things, conformable to the principles already established, in treating of the different articles to which these objects relate. If I were to discuss them again, it would be a useless repetition; and when principles are established, it is not necessary to examine one after another [cf. Montesquieu's practice in *The Spirit*] every particular case. Having therefore no new instruction to draw from this book, I shall pass to another.

One cannot affirm strongly that Destutt de Tracy's style has improved upon Montesquieu's in treating these subtleties. He would not, of course, have devoted so many pages to Montesquieu had he not seen *The Spirit* as a kind of social science landmark. And this, in effect, he says in his introductory note: "I have thought the errors of his [Montesquieu's] book the more important to be corrected, as its truths are numerous and of powerful influence on the opinions of society."

Thus the French Enlightenment and its resultant (?) Revolution do talk about Montesquieu: it would have been unthinkable that his reputation in the century should not have aroused discussion. By and large, however, the eighteenth-century opinion of Montesquieu is lean and niggardly, reluctant and apologetic. For he did not reflect clearly enough in his great work of 1748 the more radical turn of thought that characterizes most of the *philosophes* after that date, and most of the *philosophes* resent his caution. As it is eternally true that no man is a prophet in his own country, just so Montesquieu must await the nineteenth century and the post-Restoration period (*c.* 1820) for objective critical estimation in France. Meanwhile, outside his own country—and particularly in England, in the American colonies and later the United States—his fame and authority is almost immediate.

CHAPTER 5

Montesquieu Abroad

I *England*

IT was natural, perhaps, that Montesquieu's fame in England should be the first and the most resounding, that is, at least until the nineteenth century (at about the same period of his renewed fortune in France), when somehow his name is mentioned less, having receded, so to speak, into that general area of common knowledge in which we tend to forget or be unaware of the name of the man who first said or did this or that. For England clearly had played the stellar role in Montesquieu's presentation of constitutional liberty. Indeed, the first English translation was under way almost before *The Spirit* appeared in French. It was translated by a fertile translator, Thomas Nugent, already credited with the English of Dubos' *Reflexions critiques* and Burlamaqui's *Principes du droit naturel.* By 1773, Nugent's translation will have gone through ten editions; Montesquieu had written to him soon after the first edition (1750) saying that the English edition had no faults except those of the original. Thomas Gray, almost immediately upon publication in French in 1748, read the work and abandoned as now idle one of his own projects along similar lines; he wrote to his friend Thomas Wharton in 1749: "The subject . . . is as extensive as mankind; the thoughts are perfectly new, generally admirable as they are just, sometimes a little too refined . . . ; it is the gravity of Tacitus . . . tempered with the gayety and fire of a Frenchman." [1] Gray's conditioned admiration will set for the rest of the century in England the tone of comment about this authoritative work of genius, not without flaws, not the least of which, a *French* style. Goldsmith will prefer to speak of Montesquieu as a poet rather than a political scientist.

Adequate studies of Montesquieu's influence in England during the period have been made and this is not the place to recapitulate in detail.[2] It seems important, however, at least to suggest here the indubitable influence of Montesquieu on the key personalities of the period up to the end of the century: in particular, Blackstone and Edmund Burke. It is Jeremy Bentham, himself not without respect for his own debts to Montesquieu, who in the earlier years of the new century turns English thinking toward his own utilitarian line and marks the end of Montesquieu's direct influence. Yet by the old century's end, it is clear that Montesquieu's influence is already waning. A disciple of Burke, Sir James Mackintosh, sums up rather well in 1799 the shortcomings of Montesquieu's work seen by his countrymen: the uncritical use of ancient texts and traveler's accounts, the overemphasis on physical determinants, inappropriate style, etc. But Mackintosh is careful to add:

> After all . . . the *Spirit of Laws* will still remain not only one of the most solid and durable monuments of the powers of the human mind, but a striking evidence of the inestimable advantages which political philosophy may receive from a wide survey of all the various conditions of human society.[3]

It would be excessive to suggest that certain famous English works, after 1748, might not have been written without Montesquieu's example. But it is surely reasonable to believe that these works owe much to Montesquieu, as has been suggested by subsequent study. Gibbon's *Decline and Fall* (1776–88) is Montesquieu's *Grandeur et décadence des Romains* written from a quite different point of view. Adam Ferguson's *History of the Progress and Termination of the Roman Republic* (1783), written in yet another vein and limited chronologically, is still in Montesquieu's lineage. Both Gibbon[4] and Ferguson share Montesquieu's view on the Germanic origin of modern European political institutions. Ferguson's *Essay of Civil Society* (1767) had already interpreted the *Spirit of Laws* for the English public (Fletcher calls it: "Montesquieu at second-hand"). Blackstone's *Commentaries* (although probably under way in 1748) becomes the standard Anglo-Saxon text explaining Montesquieu's predilection for the English Constitution. In another field, a limited section of Montesquieu's work certainly informs a great part of Adam Smith's *Wealth of the Nations* (1776) by way of Ferguson's intermediary *Institutes of Moral Philosophy*. An isolated single parallel can instruct us here. Montesquieu had said: "A man is not poor because he has nothing, but because he does not work," to which Smith adds, "Labour alone . . . never varying in its own value is alone the ultimate and real standard by which the value of commodities can at all times and places be estimated and compared." Karl Marx will, of course, add his own variant reading but we are there far from both Montesquieu and Smith. Smith was even announced in the French press (1790) as preparing a critical examination of the *Spirit of Laws* and, although Smith's biographer, John Rae, doubts the authority behind that press release, it nonetheless exists.

Many aspects of Montesquieu's omniumgatherum will be taken up, critically to be sure, by his English colleagues: the Teutonic-feudal discussion, economic and monetary theory, education, climate, methodology, penology, slavery, colonialism, etc. But, perhaps naturally, the vital center of Montesquieu's eighteenth-century fortune in England will center about his expository recommendation of the British constitution and, in particular, the separation of powers. As Montesquieu, however, had said (and pled accordingly with his reader), all of the parts of his book are interrelated. Thus, English criticism of his separation theory must be conditioned by English evaluation of his historical method and his discussion of moral vs. physical determinants. Of the discussion on his method, one might say that English opinion is as clearly divided as is French opinion between Montesquieu and Rousseau, or between conservative and radical, between traditional and revolutionary. Thus Tory opinion would seem to call upon the authority of Montesquieu; Whig opinion on the authority of Rousseau. Yet, seen under a different lighting, before the spread of Rousseau's fame, one might have said that the liberal mind seized upon Montesquieu while the conservative seemed to cling to the statute books. There is a steady growing process in England, as Montesquieu had foreseen, and when compared to the revolutionary mind of Rousseau, Montesquieu the liberal becomes Montesquieu the conservative. That is, until the French Revolution, when, following the celebrated example of Burke, many erstwhile critics of Montesquieu rally to his point of view. In the moral-physical dialogue so important to understanding Montesquieu's thought, it is probably David Hume's opinion that encourages British thinking to attribute a preponderant influence to moral causes as determinants in jurisprudence and government.[5]

Yet, despite the serious criticism of Montesquieu's overemphasis on climate and other physical causes, a considerable portion of British opinion still attaches significant weight to physical determinants, particularly in the many discussions of colonialism attendant upon American independence and the Warren Hastings incident in East Indian affairs. In short, apart from the question of Montesquieu's having or not having properly understood the British constitution, there arises here the whole consideration of whether Montesquieu should not have seen that his thinking on that constitution was predicated as much on his metaphysical or absolute attitude to the law as upon his seemingly more significant experimental or relative attitude to the law.

In the English discussion of the separation theory, the names of Blackstone and Burke are perhaps the most well-known although Paley and DeLolme, as Fletcher shows,[6] were also important interpreters of Montesquieu in England. As early as 1749, Montesquieu had been quoted in Parliament, as his friend Barbot writes him: "The famous Pulteney, now Lord Bath I think, has quoted as authority in the English parliament, my dear Président, a passage of the *Spirit of Laws.*" [7] Mme de Tencin had written, on another occasion: "Milord Carteret used it [*Spirit*] in Parliament to uphold his opinion and to recall a law they had forgotten. He declared it was from you he had gotten the arms used by him to distinguish between legislative and executive power." [8] This is scarcely surprising, for, despite the paucity of written reviews in the English press, Bulkeley had written to Montesquieu as early as January, 1749, to say that Domville wanted Montesquieu to know that the *Spirit of Laws* (already given to Nugent for translation) "is so sought after in London . . . that booksellers have had 300 copies delivered." [9] From then on, the name of Montesquieu will very often be cited in Parliamentary debate and in written polemic as an accepted authority, and particularly in regard to the basic notion of separation of powers.

Burke (in *Thoughts on the Causes of the Present Discontents* [1770], *Reflections on the French Revolution* [1790], *Appeal from the New to the Old Whigs* [1791], and elsewhere) will often call upon Montesquieu's authority. "So complete and so pervasive," says Fletcher, "is Burke's assimilation of the ideas of Montesquieu [in *Thoughts* . . .] . . . that, in order to appreciate it fully, a reader would need to have a minute textual knowledge of the

Esprit des lois." [10] A typical comment of Burke may be cited from the debates of 1770: "If there is any principle that ought to be deeply impressed upon the minds of the members of this House, it is the principle just referred to by the honorable member [J. Harris]: Let us remember the well-known observations of the learned author of *Esprit des lois,* who states it as one of the excellencies of the English Constitution . . . that 'the judicial power is separated from the legislative. . . .'" [11]

Blackstone accepted quite naturally Montesquieu's separation of powers, although it is patent that he never wished to fix such division of powers so stringently as to justify adverse criticism that equated separation and check-and-balance with inertia. Echoing Montesquieu's words, he is nonetheless careful to add a qualifier: "[Liberty] cannot subsist long in any state unless the administration of common justice be *in some degree separated* [italics mine] from the legislative and also from the executive power . . ." [12] This interest attached particularly to the judicial (which Montesquieu had called the weakest power) is a continuing debate of consequences of the Settlement Act of 1701. Blackstone, says Janet,[13] accepts the philosophical theory of Montesquieu and adds nothing to it.

He exaggerates, perhaps; yet another Frenchman in 1824, Thomas Regnault, drew up a list of parallels between the *Commentaries* and the *Spirit of Laws.*[14] Jean de Lolme, born in Geneva, added his interpretation of the British constitution, with accompanying tribute to Montesquieu in the *Constitution de l'Angleterre* (1771). De Lolme tended, perhaps, to over-formulize the strict division between powers, unlike Blackstone, but along with the latter and Burke he helped make the English aware and proud of the existence of their constitution—in greater part thanks to earlier praise of that constitution by Montesquieu, to whom all three men admit their debt. None of them is unaware of Montesquieu's own warning that the English constitution will be corrupted when the legislative falls into the hands of the executive; that remains their chief fear (again they call Montesquieu to witness) through the parliamentary history of the last half of the eighteenth century until the French Revolution, when Burke seems to change his opinions on this score because of his fear of an all-powerful legislative without an executive in France. However aware of the inherent dangers in the system seen as dynamic rather than as De Lolme's more static check-and-balance, Burke can still echo the collective pride of many English thinkers, a pride awakened in them by Montesquieu's praise of English liberty, when he says:

What! our sublime constitution, the glory of France, the envy of the world, the pattern for mankind, the masterpiece of legislation, the collected and concentrated glory of this enlightened age! . . . Let us then consider that all these [Montesquieu's long studies] were but so many preparatory steps to qualify a man, and such a man, tinctured with no national prejudices, with no domestic affection, to admire, and to hold out to the admiration of mankind, the Constitution of England.[15]

There is a certain irony involved in the reflection that it was a French baron who crystallized English liberal opinion and rallied it behind the proven excellence of the British constitution. But this is an irony no greater than that involved in the fact that the French themselves, at the moment of the Bourbon restoration, rediscover, finally, in Montesquieu a viable theory for conservative government. The facile explanation, of course, is that we have always known that the terms liberal-conservative must be treated with caution. More to the point, this situation reflects the curious fashion in which Montesquieu by his very historical method encourages conservatism, yet by his conviction of relativity, of change and growth, encourages liberalism. In any case, Montesquieu was the natural authority for an English society in gradual transition, just as he was not the prime spokesman for French society in violent revolution during the same period. When Burke was told by Menonville that the French revolutionaries read Montesquieu, Burke found it hard to believe. "If they did," he said, "they did not understand him; and had he lived at this time [1789] he would certainly be among the refugees from France." [16] But then, Burke himself changed so radically during the experience of the French revolution that Philarète Chasles could write in mid-nineteenth century (with some exaggeration, it is true):

Friend in succession of the Foxes, the Pitts, the Windhams, the Sheridans, he is one of them and yet alone. That fine British society of the eighteenth century sees him pass through fierce struggles, proud, tender and strange; similar to the way Montesquieu passed through the philosophic school in France. Voltaire, D'Alembert, Diderot, all the heads and directors of modern destruction, denied Montesquieu. Fox and his friends could say: "Let's go eat! Burke is going to speak." [17]

There are those who would not agree with Burke and Chasles: Thomas Christie (*Letters on the Revolution of France* [1791]) and Destutt de Tracy in a letter to Burke (1790).[18] This variance is a natural consequence of possible interpretations of Montesquieu's admiration for republics coupled with his prejudice for monarchy. The things men say live after them and are subject to the vicissitudes of the times of their interpreters. Montesquieu might have spoken more clearly in a France where the press was less throttled. But that would scarcely have changed his predilections: for a republic when political virtue made it possible in a small nation; for a limited monarchy, aiming toward greater republican freedom, in a nation where a monarch and an intermediate noble class already existed—with clear warnings to both governments of the seeds of destruction within them. After 1800, Montesquieu's *Spirit* seems to speak less to the British: in part because of directions taken by their limited monarchy, in part because Montesquieu's ideas now bear the label of British minds—Blackstone, Burke, *et al.* Jeremy Bentham, to whom on one occasion Montesquieu had seemed a purveyor of "pseudo-metaphysical sophistry," and who, said Bentham, besides being abstruse and high-flown in style, had been basically misrepresented in England, could still mark the end of Montesquieu's period of direct influence with an expression of gratitude. It was Montesquieu, says Bentham, who had helped him to see the principle of utility.[19] But, somewhat like Comte with his positivism later, Bentham is too enamored of his utilitarianism to keep Montesquieu actively aboard:

> The science of legislation, though it has made but little progress, is much more simple than one could be led to believe after reading Montesquieu. The principle of utility directs all reasons to a single center: the reasons which apply to the detail of arrangements are only subordinate views of utility.[20]

Montesquieu had, certainly, his influence in other European countries during the period, as for example, upon Beccaria and prison reform in Italy,[21] on Herder and others in Germany. Yet it is particularly in English thought that his role is primary. Or one might better say Anglo-Saxon thought, for there is another country in this last half of the eighteenth century, soon to be detached from the motherland, where Montesquieu's influence is extremely important.

II *America*

Certainly one of the most tenacious academic problems among students of American civilization is to know whether at all, or to what extent, Montesquieu influenced the founding fathers as they gave birth to the United States out of this cluster of Colonies. On the one hand, the question is far from idle for historians, political and literary critics alike. On the other, it may be said, I think, with reasonable impunity, that too many pages have already been written on the subject. In 1940, Paul Spurlin published a study to which anyone interested in the problem must henceforward direct his attention.[22] Professor Spurlin does not pretend to settle the issue; he states clearly that "the immediate objective is to show the dissemination of Montesquieu's works in America." But the student who uses Spurlin's objective findings intelligently will discover in them the material for his own advised opinion.

What is perfectly clear is that Montesquieu was known in the colonies soon after publication in France, that booksellers advertised his works fairly regularly, that colleges used his *Spirit* for courses, that men famous in the first years of the new republic had read Montesquieu and quoted him on frequent occasions. Strangely enough, no work of Montesquieu was published here before 1804. That scarcely prevents his being known amongst opinion-makers, for the pattern in the book trade, even for a long time after that date, was to import titles from abroad. The two sides in the usual academic discussion on Montesquieu's role in the United States, may be described superficially as pro-French and pro-British. No doubt that until well into the nineteenth century, the new citizens remained English in their orientation and thinking; no doubt, too, that the unpredictable French in their making and nourishing a Revolution—including the Terror—were calculated to strike terror into the decent folks who now called themselves Virginians and New Englanders. No doubt, Thomas Jefferson changed his opinions over the years, and if he was a

Francophile, came to put serious limitations on his acceptance of Montesquieu's ideas around 1790. But all of this does not dismiss the possibility of French ideological influence in the formative years of the United States. The Anglophiles usually point out that it was Blackstone, rather than Montesquieu, whose influence was most felt on the founding fathers. What they should not blind us to is the very real way in which Blackstone's ideas were, to a significant degree, directed and crystallized by his knowledge of Montesquieu. Certainly, it was Blackstone who somehow managed to fit the contemporary English power structure into the mold that Montesquieu had a few years before, mistakenly, assumed to be a fact of British politics. We are also told that too many Americans took exception to too many of Montesquieu's points of view, beginning with Jefferson himself. And yet one must not say because this or that idea was unpopular, that therefore the bulk of the work was unknown and rejected. In effect, the Americans discussed Montesquieu's idea of federation much more than the famous separation of powers. Perhaps, more than the tripartite state, they discussed Montesquieu's conception of "virtue" as a principle of government. Yet whatever they discussed, sometimes with distinct aversion, we must not suppose that all of the rest of Montesquieu's writings was not present in their minds. Because an intelligent critic does not warm to a particular scene does not mean that he rejects the play out of hand; and Adams, Monroe, Madison, Jefferson, *et al.* were, all things considered, intelligent critics.

Montesquieu, Frenchman and friend of the philosophic mind, was yet far from being easily confused with the *philosophes*. Thus, on at least two scores, he was not subject to the same sterotyped judgment meted out by the Americans to most of the younger French group: he was not an atheist, and he made clear his predilection for monarchy and his distaste for violent revolution. For strange as it must appear on the surface, these Americans who had made a revolution and whose religious ideas were far from orthodox, were subject to changing reflections when the French Revolution showed them other ways of overthrowing authority, both civil and religious. More and more, toward the end of the century Montesquieu could have been accepted as the reasonable spokesman for religion (at least, morality) and civil order.

But our real interest in Montesquieu's influence centers upon the earlier years, the years of preparation and execution of the American Revolution, 1760–1789. Jefferson, who as a young man had copied out pertinent passages of Montesquieu into his *Commonplace Book,*[23] who (despite the lost evidence consequent upon the fire in his home) had works of Montesquieu listed in the subsequent first printed catalogue of his library, still had misgivings about Montesquieu at this early date because of the latter's prejudice for monarchy. Later, Jefferson will attempt to put Montesquieu in proper perspective by reducing his prestige on several grounds. Adams, who knew his Montesquieu well, criticizes particularly—a familiar song by now—the organization of the work: "Montesquieu's *Spirit of Laws,*" he says "is a very useful collection of materials; but is it too irreverent to say that it is an unfinished work?"[24] Adams underscores here what must have been a common practice of the founding fathers: i.e., they used Montesquieu as a collection of materials, quoting this or that paragraph when useful, but not reflecting too much on the novelty of some of his ideas. After all, they were still too close to Montesquieu for objectivity and it must have seemed to them after the writings of the later Frenchmen (particularly Rousseau) and later English authorities, like Blackstone, that all of Montesquieu's ideas were common wealth long in existence. Thus it is not surprising that Montesquieu's role in their ideological deliberations should appear to be minor in the records (letters, memoirs, etc.) they have left to posterity.

As we have seen, from all of Montesquieu's works, they talked most of the idea of confederation; this was natural in the years of the Articles of Confederation and the ratification of the Constitution. "The citations to Montesquieu in the Federal Convention, *The Federalist* and in the state conventions speak for themselves," says Spurlin. "Without an enumeration of the subjects of these citations, it is sufficient to point out that he was most quoted on confederate republics."[25] Even Washington shows he had read his Montesquieu on this point. But his name also appears often in discussion of the separation of powers, however much this be assumed an English rather than a French influence by certain writers. "In the endless discussion of this principle which the present investigator has encountered in the writings of Americans between 1760 and 1801," writes Spurlin, "whenever an author was named, that author with this [one] exception [William Maclay had also mentioned Locke] was always Montesquieu." But perhaps a more important, although less readily measurable, way in which Montesquieu's "spirit" called forth the "spirit" of the founding fathers was in his backbone conception of virtue and morality, as made clear by this quotation from Madison in his debates on the Constitution in the Virginia Convention. "No theoretical checks, no form of government, can render us secure; to suppose that any form of government will secure liberty or happiness without any virtue in the people, is a chimerical idea." [26] That frame of mind is far from Rousseau's *conscience* and equally far from legalistic procedures in politics coming from the English. It is pure Montesquieu, as he stands somewhat torn between ideology and reality, progress and determined cycle, optimism and pessimism.

The most concentrated period of theoretical discussion about government comes for the Americans, of course, in the struggle for acceptance of the Constitution. Whatever the final judgment of Montesquieu's role in the American experiment, the reader who has eyes and understanding cannot read *The Federalist Papers* without seeing that at several important moments in that prolonged discussion, Montesquieu enters in a vital way into the argument. Hamilton, in Letter 9, attempts to allay the fears of those purists who read too literally the "small extent" recommendation for a republic. Hamilton might have invoked here one of the ancients or the more recent Rousseau; he chooses to quote Montesquieu as recommending a small extent. And for good reason, for he continues to expose another idea of Montesquieu (and, quite rightly, underscores its overriding importance)—that of the confederate republic which, for both Montesquieu and Hamilton, combines the strength of monarchy and republic. Hamilton quotes at length from his authority: "this enlightened civilian" who has simply been misunderstood by the adversaries of the American Constitution. Madison in Letter 43, again in Letter 47, and finally in Letter 78 turns, like Hamilton, to this "oracle . . . the celebrated Montesquieu" for his authority. In Letter 43, Madison enumerates the advantages of a confederate republic forwarded by Montesquieu and, in particular, the way in which the combined states can help to quell trouble in one of the confederation. In Letter 47, Madison shows a rare comprehension for

Montesquieu's whole theory of power separation. He understands that Montesquieu may not indeed be the author of separation of powers but that it is he that interprets it most effectually; indeed he may have understood the British constitution imperfectly—it was to Montesquieu, says Madison, "what Homer has been to the didactic writers on epic poetry." Here, and in Letter 78, he leans heavily upon Montesquieu's interpretations of the three powers, in particular pointing out that separation does not mean isolation and concurring with Montesquieu's appraisal of the judiciary as the weakest of the three powers. Parrington may say if he likes that "in elaborating a system of checks and balances the members of the convention were influenced by the practical considerations of economic determinism more than by the theories of Montesquieu," and with some justification; he nonetheless has obscured the truth for two generations of students of American studies.

Any attempt at reaching a conclusion on the dimensions of Montesquieu's contribution to the founding of the United States of America must, it seems to me, comprehend that the important issue is not whether Montesquieu had drawn his conclusions validly from his readings (he does not in the case of England), nor whether his every word is taken uncritically by the Americans (it is not). Montesquieu, in many ways, created in theory the government (confederate republic with formal separation of powers) that the Americans came closest to infusing with reality. It is a classic example of vision (Montesquieu's spirit) becoming flesh (the American Constitution). Thus, the important consideration is *not* whether Montesquieu had spelled out all that eventually becomes the Constitution, but that, out of his vast erudition and dynamic theories, he was *taken* for the authority needed when the Americans applied the spirit of laws to the making of laws.

CHAPTER 6

Nineteenth-Century Opinion

SINCE we tend to use such language as "precursor," "father of," "founder of," etc., somewhat loosely, it has always remained a moot point whether or not we shall drape upon Montesquieu's shoulders the mantle of precursor or father of French social studies. Without debating the issue, let us assume that by his very historical moment, he may be called a precursor, however important a one. A similar problem arises if we push into the nineteenth century. Is it Comte or Durkheim whom we should consider the father of French social science? The question is certainly not idle; let us, however, simply say that what both Comte and Durkheim may have had to say of Montesquieu must interest us profoundly if we are to assay French opinion of *The Spirit* among those intellectual workers closest to Montesquieu: the social scientists, and not as some might have it, the historians or the political scientists. For the vineyards in which Montesquieu was, sometimes perhaps unconsciously, laboring were not then so clearly demarcated, and we need the more general term. Montesquieu would no doubt have thought of himself as working in the humanities or the human sciences with an occasional foray into natural science.

I *Comte*

Auguste Comte (1798–1857), born like Victor Hugo at the turning of the century, is considered by most Frenchmen the father of social science. His great work, *A Course in Positive Philosophy*, although not now widely read and known, is nonetheless a philosophic landmark of the century. His basic idea was that mankind had, necessarily and naturally, passed through two prior stages: the mythological and the metaphysical, and was only now (after the Enlightenment and the Revolution) entering into a third and final stage which he calls positivistic. The central concept behind that word suggests scientific method and social progress. Thus what Comte had to say about Montesquieu will be indicative of his reputation among post-Enlightenment thinkers.

Comte never devoted a full essay to Montesquieu, but in his 47th lesson (Vol. IV of the *Course*) he devotes several pages to those thinkers who had come before him and, in a sense, prepared positivism. Strangely, he admits of very few true precursors. Amongst the ancients perhaps there is Aristotle, but in effect none of the ancients can really qualify because they turned almost entirely to the past as being a golden age and because mankind was simply not ready for the positivistic stage. Pascal is given a brief commendation *en passant,* not because he came anywhere close to positivist ideals but because, being a mathematician like Comte, he had the vision to write the following: "The whole succession of men during the long course of centuries, must be considered as a single man, who subsists and learns continually." Yet Pascal was without that other faith, pointed toward the future, which Comte considers the *sine qua non* of positivist thought. Without the fundamental notion of progress, one lacks the first necessary base of all true social science. "The first and most important series of studies which appear as directly destined to found, finally, social science, is thus the work of the great Montesquieu, first in his treatise on Roman politics and especially in his *Spirit of Laws.*"

Comte admires Montesquieu's opening pages and the general definition he gives to law. Thereafter he is less enthusiastic and finds the long series of paragraphs, judgments, and excursions into varied subjects singularly unconnected to any "truly scientific development." Montesquieu simply does not follow through on the great promise we sense in the beginning of his work. Among other things, the English system is not what Montesquieu thought it was and is not representative of the type of free government as he thought. The "only portion which can present a certain effective positivity" is Montesquieu's discussion of climatic determinants, but, says Comte, he tends to exaggerate. Climate cannot change the direction, it can change only the rate of progression.

One might suppose, then, that Comte thinks very little of Montesquieu's contribution. On the contrary, there are sufficient historical reasons to explain the weakness of his work. But there is no easy explanation for the great genius Montesquieu showed in his original concept: that political phenomena are as necessarily subject to invariable natural law as are physical phenomena. Montesquieu was doomed to failure in enlarging on his basic concept because (1) he tried to submit social phenomena to positive spirit before there was sufficient biological knowledge and (2) he tried to reorganize social thinking in a historic moment ripe for a revolution he did not understand. The reality of the coming revolution, says Comte, was much better understood by that "simple sophist Rousseau." Montesquieu "can be fully appreciated only by our [Comte's] posterity in which the finally perfected extension of positive philosophy to the whole ensemble of social speculations, will make deeply felt the high value of his [Montesquieu's] precocious experiments." Those premature excursions into virgin territory have, nonetheless, contributed to putting properly the general question that is one day to be solved by social science.

The only other philosopher of the Enlightenment cited by Comte is Condorcet, who grasped better, coming later, the revolutionary spirit. Both men fail to qualify as social scientists but they build on that necessary foundation of historic fact. One cannot but admire the deep philosophic superiority of Montesquieu, says Comte in conclusion, who somehow understood how to free himself from "the critical prejudices that dominated all thinking of his contemporaries" and which we can discern in Montesquieu's own youthful works. Montesquieu, therefore, claims right of citizen in the much later land of the social sciences for having followed his vision at a time when that vision appeared to be a kind of folly, and that despite the perfectly understandable shortcomings of much of his major work.

II *Durkheim*

Durkheim's Latin thesis on Montesquieu is a kind of landmark in the social sciences. The text, printed in 1892 at Bordeaux, was dedicated to Fustel de Coulanges.[1] It can be translated as *What Secondat (Montesquieu) contributed to the Foundation of the Social Sciences.*

Durkheim points out in his introduction that the French have taken for granted that the whole discipline of the social sciences is alien to France. Great as may be English and German contributions (Spencer, Bagehot, Schaeffle, etc.), it still remains true, says Durkheim, that it was a Frenchman, Montesquieu, who had established the principles of that science. Montesquieu treated only a segment of sociology—laws. But his method is valid for other social studies, although, naturally, it lacked most of the tools for sociological research now commonly accepted. Montesquieu, says Durkheim, gave to social science a consciousness of its nature, direction, and material.

It was Montesquieu, according to Durkheim, who unlike his contemporaries made it clear that social facts were natural things (in the nature of things) and not dependent on human will as distinct from nature. Unlike Montesquieu, his contemporaries told us not what is, but what ought to be. Montesquieu, for example, did not make preference or excellence of a particular sort of government the object of his studies. Durkheim, objecting to Montesquieu's organization, insists on the distinction between type of society and type of state; the role of the social sciences is to classify these disparate things. And they are social things not individual things; social science is not psychology. One of Montesquieu's virtues, if not to have made a firm separation of different entities is his work, is to pass easily from science to art, from fact to moral.

In discussing laws, Montesquieu, unlike his predecessors, does not make a single certain kind of law natural, and others dependent on human will; he seeks the spirit of all laws in their derivation from natural law, says Durkheim. Society thus, as an entity, derives from nature, naturally. What Montesquieu did not do was to push forward into showing the individual life as a result of social life. The tradition of his times was still too strong to encourage such a break.

As to societies, Durkheim sees that Montesquieu seems to be talking of governments, not of types of society. Yet in his division into republic (democracy and aristocracy), monarchy, and despotism and in his description of them, his thinking is more along the lines of types of society than forms of government. Thus, for example, it does not suffice to describe a monarchy as the rule of a single person, but rather as a society in which various classes keep to their demarcated duties and privileges, motivated by class *honor* rather than by common concern for the *rem publicam*, which distinguishes the republic. The laws, then, are determined by the type of society: ". . . from the size of a nation, from the configuration of the land it occupies, from the nature of soil and climate, one can deduce to which sort that society belongs and what are its laws and institutions" says Durkheim, summing up Montesquieu.

But there is another side to Montesquieu's doctrine, says Durkheim, and it seems a contradiction to the above. This contradiction will enlighten us on the difficulties Montesquieu met with in his century and those still confronting the establishment of the social sciences. For the laws that seemed to derive from the nature of things are also, according to Montesquieu, produced by the legislator, understanding the nature of things, and writing the laws in a certain fashion commensurate with the kind of society. Here there would seem to be confusion between what is naturally necessary and what is morally desirable, between nature and reason. Durkheim concludes that: "if . . . with Montesquieu the notion of natural law does not extend to the social life entire, it nevertheless applies to the greater part. If his work still keeps to the ancient confusion between art and science . . . this weakness is manifested only occasionally."

Durkheim next discusses Montesquieu's method, and, like so many other critics, sees a peculiar combination of deductive and experimental, with a decided leaning still in Montesquieu, despite the vast comparative study of facts, toward deduction ". . . instead of using deduction to interpret what has been proven by experience, he uses rather experience to clarify . . . the conclusions of deduction." "In a word, Montesquieu did not sufficiently understand how much, as Bacon says, the finesse of things escapes the finesse of the human mind: and this explains why he has such confidence in reason and deduction." Despite the basic confusion of the method, Durkheim gives Montesquieu copious credit for having understood that everything is interrelated in the social sciences and that the economist, political theorist, moralist, etc., cannot work in isolation in their "disciplines." Notwithstanding, Durkheim then finds that Montesquieu was singularly unaware of the concept of progress: i.e., in social studies, that societies grow one out of the other and eventually, from underdeveloped to developed, find a higher form of social organization.

One may conclude that Durkheim makes a serious and sincere attempt to give to Montesquieu the credit he deserves for having "established the fundamental principles of social science," particularly by his insistence on types and laws. He is perhaps, at times, a little severe in his criticism of Montesquieu's method as well as in his estimate of Montesquieu's notion of progress. He shows, equitably, that both Montesquieu and Comte contributed something essential to social science, although each only a part of the truth. He is eminently generous in attributing to Montesquieu all of what later constitutes *sociology,* except the name. But, as is perhaps natural between workers in the two disciplines of the humanities and the social sciences, he tends to see as weakness all that is humanism in Montesquieu since it detracts from the full application of the social scientific method. His essay remains one of the most serious and sympathetic analyses of Montesquieu's contribution to man's knowledge of himself.

III *Lanson*

Another of the historically important articles on Montesquieu was written by that dean of French literary critics who spans the close of the nineteenth and the beginning of the twentieth centuries, Gustave Lanson. In a former article (1896), Lanson had attempted to show that Montesquieu's lack of order springs from Montesquieu's direct application of the Cartesian method. In the article considered here (1916), Lanson attempts to reconcile that seeming paradoxical presence in the *Spirit* of what he calls "historic determinism" and "social idealism." As Lanson says, there is little doubt that Montesquieu had shown a distinct idealism in *The Persian Letters* and in key passages of *The Spirit;* he underlines quite rightly Montesquieu's vocabulary with its "must" and "ought to." Yet in his historical studies, Montesquieu would seem to show that great men are more acted upon than actors.

Lanson attempts to show that there is essentially no contradiction, or rather that Montesquieu's conciliation of these contraries was a first step in establishing political science. Montesquieu fused in himself what later Auguste Comte will consider as two stages: the objective elaboration of truth and the practical application of truth. Skirting the problem of fatalism-determinism, Lanson holds that "human will, by positing a law, creates new relationships from which results new necessity." The art of lawmaking, in Montesquieu's mature thought, becomes the art of putting aside necessity and utilizing determinism to the advantage of idealism. For, says Lanson, to Montesquieu the physical world and the moral world are two, and although physical necessity implies existence, moral necessity need not imply existence. He tries to gauge Montesquieu's true contribution to all subsequent social and political science as based essentially on the solution he brings to the determinist-idealist paradox. "His true thought," concludes Lanson, "unites tradition and progress, the people and its leaders, and places the conservative spirit as well as the scientific spirit at the service of idealistic reform."

CHAPTER 7

Conclusion

It is always difficult, and, many times, unfair to conclude. Montesquieu wrote, when all is said, three books; he was not prolific in the age of Voltaire, Rousseau, and Diderot. Yet his name elicits and should elicit some reaction from every commonly cultured Occidental.

The Persian Letters stands as a literary landmark and influences thinking about the novel for a good part of the century. It can be read with pleasure today, but the book scarcely coincides with the modern reader's notion of the novel. The study on the Romans filled an important need in Montesquieu's intellectual formation and provided a pleasant compendium of Roman history for his contemporaries. But it has been superseded many times over by more methodical histories and by better informed studies that have taken advantage of continuing research. The modern student of history would turn to it only after having finished Gibbon and that feat, in itself, remains doubtful. The great work on the laws is again and most indubitably a landmark, but at the risk of attack for cynicism, it may be doubted that more than a handful of social scientists in any given academic institution have read it in its entirety. All of this is not to belittle the reputation of a great man. But let us try to be honest in our estimate of why greatness still attaches to his name.

It will seem ungracious, at the very least, to voice here a regret, a regret as unreasonable as the criticisms levied against Montesquieu by his contemporaries for not having written *The Spirit* as they would have done. The regret is simply that Montesquieu spent twenty years on his great work and then stopped writing, never returning to the rich vein in him so clearly demonstrated by the *Persian Letters*. Or, to put it in another fashion, the literary man cannot but regret that Montesquieu's faltering vision saw his future solely in scholarship and not in the novel. For had he worked in that direction (discounting the *Temple of Cnidus,* which even he knew was a momentary detour), he would no doubt have added important titles to a century already rich with *La Nouvelle Héloise, Candide,* and *Le Neveu de Rameau,* to mention the fictional achievements of only the *philosophes.* But such regret is surely wrong-headed and perhaps, on the contrary, we should be grateful that the man who wrote the *Spirit* was the same man who *might have written* a great novel—and that for a very good reason. The reader who has digested *The Spirit* has lived a rare intellectual experience. He has just as surely missed much if he has not looked into the travel-notes and the *Pensées,* that heteroclite collection of aphorisms, character sketches, and intimate reflection. They are eminently human and that is the very good reason one must be grateful that their author wrote *The Spirit.* Dry as dust as much of *The Spirit* material might have been, Montesquieu's personality still comes through.

That this very fact has been and continues to be one of the chief sources of criticism of his work has been shown above. It must be seen, rather, it seems to me, as a particular reason for the lasting quality of the *Spirit.* For Montesquieu never forgot for one moment that what he was really talking about was a man—men living together to be sure, but fundamentally a man. However important it has since become that social scientists should emulate the objectivity of their confrères in the natural sciences, this single facet, the humanity of Montesquieu, is still the first to catch the eye of the modern reader. For him, the science of society was predicated upon the knowledge and comprehension of the human being, and who says comprehension says sympathy. If Montaigne, in that eminently French way of uncomplicated self-analysis, could hope to know himself, Montesquieu would seem to progress along the same road by proposing to extrapolate social self from a multitude of historical selves. Ste.-Beuve, that usually penetrating and sagacious judge of men, writers, and thinkers, somehow underestimates Montesquieu's essential honesty and credits him with the illusion that his eighteenth-century colleagues had criticized him for. "I have stated the radical defect that I believe is in Montesquieu's statesmanship; he puts the average of humanity, considered in its natural data, rather higher than it is." If Montesquieu put that humanity higher, he did so advisedly. How blind the extraordinary vision of Ste.-Beuve can become on occasion is even more apparent in the following estimate of Montesquieu as "one of those gods who are benefactors of humanity without human tenderness."

Montesquieu's historical method was, of course, not eventually aimed at presenting a series of psychological sketches, however much the individual human being remained his measure. He hoped, like many other historians of his day, to use the past in order to enlighten the future. That was normal and natural and one of the accepted uses of history. But Montesquieu uses history in two other ways that characterize his peculiar method immediately. If the study of historical civilizations gave him valuable information on various systems of social living and, hence, a realization of the basic relativity obtaining in human affairs, he nonetheless continued to impose on that experience the conviction that there could be an absolute discerned in the relative. However varied in detail, each historical society had to disclose eventually a common Reason at work. He was to be harshly criticized for such thinking, which seemed to most of his readers to confuse the inductive with the deductive, as we have seen above. Yet he persisted in supposing that diversity itself continued to reveal a natural reason behind all social organization. Secondly, once he had, as he puts it, found his principles, he is careful not to fix them adamantly for all time. For his vision of the historical process is a dynamic one, conscious of change, development, and the on-going process. "Its function," remarks Fletcher, "is not historical but prophetic." [1] Thus, even his theory of check and balance and the separation of powers could never have been stated in the static formalization of a De Lolme. Nor, with all of his advised hope for human progress as more and more could be known of the spirit behind social organization, could he have accepted Auguste Comte's later conviction that progress was a one-way street; he had been, since the Troglodytes, too aware of ever-imminent regression. Indeed he had warned his prize society, the English, of such dangers in terms which became meaningful to most late eighteenth-century English thinkers. Thus Bentham, who dismisses Montesquieu all too easily because he did not show that legislation was a simple matter (i.e., so long as it set its sights irrevocably on utilitarianism) might, posthumously and in the spirit world, have been dismissed by Montesquieu, who was ever conscious of the difficulty of balancing all possible determinants to arrive at just legislation. Montesquieu would first have wanted to know "useful for whom?" and thereby he returns us to one of the basic intentions of his twenty-year work. "Several people," he writes in his notes, "have examined which is better: monarchy, aristocracy or the popular state. But, as there are an infinity of kinds of monarchy, aristocracy and popular state, the question thus stated is so vague that one would have to possess very little logic to want to treat it." [2]

The Reason behind diversity and relativity, the natural law behind the positive, Montesquieu had sought to clarify in those first concentrated pages (the metaphysical pages, as his adverse critics will have it). Years of meditation go into that famous definition—general enough to be universal, specific enough to accommodate the diversity of positive laws: laws are relationships deriving from the nature of things. Curiously, Montesquieu does not insist much in his work on the applicability of that definition to so-called laws of science: gases, volumes, planetary movement, etc. And yet he must have seen his definition as applicable to both human law and scientific law, both somehow emerging from an overriding natural law. Here is where Goldsmith and others so easily see the poet in Montesquieu: given other times and other concerns, Montesquieu's *Spirit* might have become *De Rerum Natura* or *La Divina Commedia.* One can best judge Montesquieu's definition by comparing it with more modern thinking on the subject. Justice Cardozo gave the following as his definition of law. "A principle or rule of conduct so established as to justify a prediction with reasonable certainty that it will be enforced by the courts if its authority is challenged is a principle or rule of law." [3] This is a legalist definition and tells us little of the spirit behind the law. Just so, in general, American law as taught and practised has been almost exclusively a "case" approach, a natural outcome of the preponderant influence of English law with its precedent and handbook by Blackstone. Oddly, we have seen how much the *Commentaries* partake of Montesquieu. Malinowski described civil law as "the positive law governing all the phases of tribal life [consisting] . . . of a body of binding obligations, regarded as a right by one party and acknowedged as a duty by the other, kept in force by a specific mechanism of a reciprocity and publicity inherent in the structure of their society." [4]

Here we have a social scientist's (anthropologist's) definition, exact, no doubt, in its reference frame. But again, we know very little of the "specific mechanism" or of the "structure of society in which it inheres," very little, again, of the spirit of the law or of the way in which "their" society corresponds to ours or yours.

These are very likely questions no longer to be asked for they tend to cross disciplines. And were Montesquieu to write his study today, he would no doubt suffer the disdain of his colleagues in many disciplines who would not choose to bite off so much. All that is very well and understandable in a world that has made specialization a necessity, or attempted to convince us that it is a necessity. Yet Montesquieu, feeling his way where none had gone before in precisely his tracks, insisted upon treating of the spirit behind the law, thus involving himself in history, philosophy, psychology, anthropology, geography, economics, linguistics, sociology, political science, demography, etc. and all the resultant branches of intermarriage like economic geography, sociology of knowledge, linguistic anthropology, and the like. Foolish (from the modern point of view) he no doubt was, but then, very brave, too, as Janet has pointed out. Critics might have done better, he says, to "point out in detail the vast expanse and obscurity of the subject chosen by him and the power of mind with which he mastered it." [5] Montesquieu speaks to this point for himself well, and with his usual sincere (as opposed to false) humility. He replies to his friend Solar's ecstatic praise of his great work (and he knew its worth) in the following terms:

> It is true that the subject is fine and great; I must fear that it was greater than myself. I can say that I have worked at it all my life: upon finishing college, I had put into my hands books of law; I sought out their spirit, I toiled, I did nothing worthwhile. Twenty years ago I discovered my principles: they are very simple; another man having worked as much as I, would have done better than I did. But I must admit that this work just about killed me; I am going to rest, I shall work no more.[6]

Huntington Cairns, in his general work on law and the social sciences, in a passage not specifically on Montesquieu, seems kinder to Montesquieu than many of his predecessors. "It has been found," he says, "that real progress in the law lies in patiently working backwards toward the source of legal rules instead of beginning with a hypothesis and working forward, attempting at the same time to make each apparent advance conform with the hypothesis." [7] He could not have better spelled out Montesquieu's method, for Montesquieu's hypothesis (his discovery of his principles, as he puts it) comes only after considerable working backwards toward the source. Cairns also recalls, at another point, the *Interpretations of Legal History* (1923) of Pound: "The fundamental idea of the common law is, as Pound has shown, relation not will." [8] That fundamental idea might have been lifted with only a change in language from Montesquieu's most cherished conclusion, the one that finally dictates his general definition of law: *rapport* from the nature of things and not *volonté* from the accidental and individual.

It will appear to some sophomoric to reduce the reasons for Montesquieu's great contribution to Western thought to just two; let it appear so. If we leave aside the details (all of them instructive), Montesquieu is telling us that (1) laws all spring from the nature of things, no matter how far removed therefrom some specific laws may appear and (2) that, although there is somewhere, and ill-understood as yet, a common spirit of all law, the specific laws, of various kinds and nature, are all relative rather than absolute, and relative to so many determinants that our work of clarification, even in the twentieth century, has only begun. Thus, we are wrong to suppose that the English constitution was the end point of Montesquieu's search. It just happened that, at that time, the English constitution with its separation of powers seemed to have achieved the greatest share of liberty. It is liberty that is important and the key to his long studies, not the British constitution. Indeed, with his realistic (as some say, pessimistic) vision, he foresaw the direction in which the British constitution would most likely be weakened: the usurpation of the legislative by the executive. Strangely enough, it is the opposite that has taken place in England: continual strengthening of the legislative over the executive, a movement foreseen by Montesquieu in any government at a given time and a *progression* toward republicanism as long as republicanism did not beget mob rule. Curiously, it is in England's offspring, the United States, that the contrary development would seem to be steadily developing: a gradual strengthening of the executive over the legislative. A constitution for Montesquieu, then, is not *per se* sacrosanct but rather represents the most developed form of safeguard against the ever-threatening cycle of the Troglodytes. Clearly, for Montesquieu, the best constitution was that one which allowed for change within its existing form. For supposing that the principle did not change, the constitution would continue to reflect that principle through numerous specific and temporary interpretations of the document. If the principle were to change (political virtue in the case of the United States) then the constitution would be less than worthless, and would lead to situations analogous to those in Roman history where the republic labored in vain to tie old laws (and customs) to decadent principle. A constitution, then, is not sacred, but it should be durable while allowing for interpretation; the only other alternative is anarchy. Better continual change that can be read into the existing constitution than violent revolution and chaos.

Whether future social scientists will continue to claim Montesquieu as colleague or precursor remains to be seen. That his broad venture strikes some of them as superficial can be no surprise, given the broadened field of knowledge in those sciences.[9] Robert Flint (*Philosophy of History . . .*) in 1874 had already spelled out what was for him Montesquieu's weakness:

> It was that of ignoring the relation not only of one law to another, but of one stage of law to another, and of the relation of each stage and system of law to coexistent and contemporaneous stages and systems of religion, art, science and industry. Social phenomena such as laws are, cannot be explained like the merely physical phenomena of natural philosophy and chemistry.[10]

But the humanist must beg leave to essay the conclusion that Montesquieu was one of the last scientists of society to cling to his conviction during every waking hour that the all was in the all and that the spirit behind the law, as behind every social discipline, was by definition human. The science of society was to Montesquieu the science of man, in all his varied aspects and only the all could keep in communication with the many-faceted complications of human life—physical and mental. He would have been the first to deplore the necessity for specialization; he would have been the first to encourage a constant meeting point, man, for the specialists. In a rather discouraging entry of his notes, he foresees how easy it can be to lose sight of the forest for the trees: "People of parts," he warns, "who have read a lot, often fall into disdain for everything." [11] That is certainly a pitfall he escaped, although he must have known the ease with which he could have fallen. As for the findings he gleaned, he is aware that he, like other researchers and scholars, can be tempted to erect therefrom a system and have Truth stamped once and for all, or at least be able to state categorically that such and such is normal and preferable, such and such decadent and to be discouraged. Certainly there are preferences we may want to hold but we must be certain of their interrelationship to the all, must realize how rarely all men of good will and good intellect can accept a common preference. "The terms beautiful, good, noble, great and perfect," he says in his notes, this time in the language of his younger *philosophe* colleagues, "are attributes of objects, relative to the beings who consider them." [12] Add to that, the findings of *The Spirit* that inform us as to the diversity of determinants of those "beings who consider," and the dimensions of man's eventual knowledge of himself and his world become clear.

That is why, weary to the bone and almost completely blind toward the end, his "soul" continued "to be seized by everything." That is why on many scores, he passes in his enthusiasm to moments when his critical sense wavers; that is why a good part of the details of his insistence on physical and climatic determinants has been discounted, although the basic idea has been further developed by many: Mme de Staël, Herder, Ratzel, Vidal de la-Blache, Miss Churchill Simple, etc. That is why our hearts fill with a kind of pride in another human mind that was seized with the basic injustice of slavery and cognizant of the abuses of colonialism, back there in the eighteenth century when normal souls did not allow themselves to be aroused by such long established institutions; institutions, let Montesquieu continue to remind us, are not necessarily the nature of things.[13]

Finally, that is why we are privileged and delighted to have record of some of the things that seized Montesquieu's soul yet never quite belonged in *The Spirit*. Even when he is wrong, he is delightful, and one finds it difficult to imagine the serious social scientist who could write the following even in his notes:

> Who would have wanted to get married if concubinage were permitted?
>
> It's men you have to push into marriage, not girls.
>
> Scaramouche [*commedia dell'arte*] is crying. They ask him why. He says: "Il mondo s'imputanisce, ed io son vecchio." It is his naiveté that amuses besides his expression.
>
> Friendship is a contract by which we agree to perform little favors for someone so that he will perform big ones in return.
>
> Remedy for dropsy.—I found it in some old papers of my forefathers: Take a pint of red wine quite sour, a half pound of olive oil and a pinch of rosemary. Boil all together in an earthenware pot, brand new and varnished if possible. Boil down to half, then, pour it all through fine white cloth. This gives a syrup. You will use it, lukewarm, and rub the patient wherever he is swollen, applying very hot towels. Use twice every day until cured. The remedy is foolproof.[14]

"Mon âme se prend à tout." That is the best explanation of our *président*, no longer the stern purveyor of dry stuff he has too often been taken for. We are, perhaps, too far removed from the eighteenth century to take such a fellow seriously—ladies' man, *président*, book-worm, writer of angry notes,[15] amateur of home remedies, etc. Yet that is surely the portrait we must keep of him if we are to understand his method, his intention, and his message. He is the ideal scholar to a point now too often forgotten in our busy and separate disciplines.

> If the work is good, it belongs to everyone; if it is written about important matters, it is fitting that all good minds help authors with their remarks and reflections. The truths that I find belong to you and those you find belong to me. Truth is like the sea which Mr. Locke calls the great commune of the universe; it is only through the reason of others that one becomes oneself reasonable.[16]

That is, in little, the same Reason that Montesquieu sensed behind the all—not mathematical reason, not Descartes' reason (much as Montesquieu admired him), but, in the final analysis, reasonableness. Yet that reasonableness of the One of which all things partake must not blind us to the complications of the all in all. Montesquieu, among his other achievements, was an excellent traveler, as is clear from his travel notes. It is one of those notes that perhaps best catches the man, his controversial method, and the knowledge toward which he worked so hard and long:

> When I arrive in a city, I always go upon the highest church steeple or tower, to see the whole together before seeing all the parts; and, as I leave the city I do the same, to fix my ideas.[17]

Notes and References

CHAPTER ONE

Abbreviations: *NRF: Oeuvres complètes* (Gallimard); *Nagel: Oeuvres complètes* (Nagel).

1. "I am going to begin by a stupid thing which is my genealogy." *NRF*, I, 989.

2. *président à mortier*—one of the chief officers of a *parlement*, the sovereign court of justice in various districts or regions of France before the Revolution. The function of the *parlement* was to record edicts of the king. The *premier président* was the ranking officer. The *mortier* was the hat worn by a *président*, honorary sign of his office. It might be said to resemble a *round* model of the mortar-board, familiar to American academic life. Bordeaux was the important *parlement* for the southwest of France (Guyenne).

3. Later in life, as becomes clear from his correspondence, Montesquieu considered steps toward elevating Montesquieu to a marquisate; thus several of his friends during a certain period address him as marquis de Montesquieu. See *Nagel*, III, Letters # 233, 280, 281, and note (b), p. 950.

4. "When I see Louis XIV, led about by the Jesuits, send off to his enemies subjects, soldiers, merchants, workers, his commerce and expel the Huguenots, I have more pity for him than for the Huguenots." *NRF*, I, 1390.

5. "I am going to draw a rather stupid thing: my portrait." *NRF*, I, 975.

6. *NRF*, I, 975.

7. "Mon âme se prend à tout." Letter to Maupertuis, 1746. *Nagel*, III, 1072.

8. *NRF*, I, 978.

9. *NRF*, I, 976 and 983.

10. *NRF*, I, 979.

11. *NRF*, I, 978.

12. His correspondence gives scant, although provocative testimony on his marriage. "I shall remain here for another few months, in love with my woods, my garden, my solitude and my wife," he writes

about life at La Brède in 1725. A rare letter from his wife (1742–43) bears witness to her constant and, perhaps one-sided, love: "Adieu, my dear friend, I love you a hundred times more than you love me; you will see by this that I am quite generous, I should not be so if you merited it less. . . . I kiss you with all my heart. I shall not write to you for another year, if you do not write me." *Nagel,* III, 792 and 1032. But, perhaps this seeming neglect is but a reflection of Montesquieu's absent-mindedness, for which he was apparently famous amongst his friends (*Nagel,* III, 828, note).

13. *NRF,* I, 978.

14. Cf. Barbot, in a letter of 1726: "Even the clever columnists do not hesitate to think it is you [Montesquieu tried to keep the preliminary steps in the sale a secret] and it will no doubt soon be public knowledge; whoever it is wanting to sell the position is condemned strongly and indiscriminately by the people"; *Nagel,* III, 825. The decision to sell thus had to cope with public opinion.

15. See *NRF,* I, 977. Also, Barbot gives a notion of the demands of the post in a letter: "The job at the Palace is not amusing, I admit. But much of it falls into routine; it will scarcely take you from other occupations and pleasures and, if you were willing to come down to these matters one hour a day . . ." *Nagel,* III, 819.

16. *NRF,* I, 976. For additional examples, *Nagel,* III, 830–31; *NRF,* I, 975 sqq. An apparently favorite closing to his love notes, used on several ladies, was: "Ma chère petite, je crois que si je te tenois, je mourrois dans tes bras."

17. *NRF,* I, 981–982. See also *Nagel,* III, 776.

18. *NRF,* I, 983.

19. See the firm letters written by the "master" of La Brède concerning presumptuous servants: *Nagel,* III, 1042–3, 1050; e.g., ". . . the first time I hear such talk I shall have him tossed into prison"; or the curious fragment of a letter to some unknown official in which the easy-going Montesquieu becomes unusually firm: "Monsieur—I don't give a bloody damn for you, your wife, your family, and all the lackeys who, by dint of rascality have become tax-farmers"; *Nagel,* III, 829.

20. *NRF,* I, 981.

21. "As for me, my only regimen is to diet when I have committed excess, to sleep when I have stayed up late, not to be worried by disappointment, pleasure, work or loafing." *NRF,* I, 983.

22. *Nagel,* III, 728.

23. Claude Boucher, *intendant de Bordeaux, NRF,* I, 1579. Also see *Nagel,* III, 263 and 871.

24. For Montesquieu's witty projects of setting a marker to commemorate his victory (finally in 1743) over the Jurats, see *NRF,* I, 987–88.

25. *NRF*, I, 999.
26. *NRF*, I, 1001.
27. Montesquieu to Maupertuis in a letter of 25 November, 1746. *Nagel*, III, 1072.
28. *NRF*, I, 613; "Here the walls have tongues."
29. *NRF*, I, 539.
30. *NRF*, I, 548.
31. Ibid.
32. *NRF*, I, 552.
33. *NRF*, I, 559.
34. *NRF*, I, 601.
35. *NRF*, I, 607.
36. *NRF*, I, 624.
37. Ibid.
38. *NRF*, I, 701.
39. *NRF*, I, 671.
40. *NRF*, I, 721.
41. *NRF*, I, 806.
42. *NRF*, I, 820.
43. *NRF*, I, 863.
44. *NRF*, I, 865.
45. *NRF*, I, 869.
46. *NRF*, I, 874.
47. *NRF*, I, 876.
48. *NRF*, I, 877.
49. *NRF*, I, 884.
50. "I adopted the resolution to read only good books: the man who reads bad ones is like a man who passes his life in bad company." *NRF*, I, 996.
51. A partial list of such comparative studies follows: "Montesquieu et J. B. Vico" by Jules Chaix-Ruy; *Montesquieu et la tradition politique anglaise en France; les sources anglaises de l'Esprit des Lois* by Joseph Dedieu; "Platon et Montesquieu, théoriciens politiques" by Jacques Flach; *Montesquieu e Machiavelli* by Ettore Levi-Malvano; "Montesquieu and Machiavelli" by Robert Shackleton; *Machiavel et Montesquieu* by Marc Duconseil; *Le Spinozisme de Montesquieu* by Charles Oudin; "Montesquieu, Bolingbroke and the Separation of Powers" by Robert Shackleton; "La filosofia politica in Montesquieu ed Aristotele" by Luigi Ferri.
52. *NRF*, II, 231.
53. Montesquieu writes to Blackwell (translator of Plato) in 1751: "The work that you have given to the public is perhaps the one I have the most desired all my life, because I believe that philosopher is the one whose writings have been most useful to me; he is the angels' phil-

osopher and even more so the philosopher for men, for he taught them the dignity of their nature." *Nagel,* III, 1407.

54. Quoted in Dedieu, *Montesquieu, l'homme et l'oeuvre,* p. 82–83.

55. "Quand une république est corrompue, on ne peut remédier à aucun des maux qui naissent, qu'en ôtant la corruption et en s'appelant les principes." *Spirit,* VIII, 12 (*NRF,* II, 359). "E cosa piu chiara che la luce, che non si rinovando questi corpi, non durono. Il modo di rinovargli è. . . . ridurgli verso i principii suoi." *Discorsi,* III, i. See above, note 51.

56. R. Shackleton, "Montesquieu and Machiavelli."

57. See *NRF,* 1251 sqq. for some typical comments of Montesquieu on Voltaire.

58. Pierre Coste (1668–1747) also wrote assiduously on Montaigne. Montesquieu leaves us an interesting and ever valid comment on the scholar: "M. Coste (I said laughing) thinks he invented Montaigne, and he blushes when people praise Montaigne in his presence." *NRF,* I, 1254.

59. See on this subject: Joseph Dedieu, *Montesquieu et la tradition politique anglaise en France;* Robert Shackleton, "Montesquieu, Bolingbroke and the Separation of Powers."

60. *NRF,* II, 1038.

CHAPTER TWO

1. "I have the disease of making books and then being ashamed of them when I have finished them." *NRF,* I, 997.

2. "I have ever seen that, to succeed completely in society, one must appear wise and be a fool." *NRF,* I, 1271.

3. Montesquieu was conscious of the etymologies of the two terms (despot and tyrant) and uses them accordingly, never interchangeably.

4. Paul Valéry, *Variété,* II.

5. See R. L. Cru, edition of *Lettres persanes* (New York: Oxford, 1914); Elie Carcassonne, edition of same (Paris: Roches, 1929); Charles Vellay, "La Genèse de l'Esprit des Lois"; Camille Jullian, edition of *Romains* (Paris: Hachette, 1923).

6. See below, page 73.

7. See, in particular, Alessandro S. Crisafulli, "Parallels to ideas in the *Lettres persanes,*" in *PMLA,* 1937.

8. *NRF,* I, 1245.

9. See Pauline Kra, "The Invisible Chain of Montesquieu's *Lettres persanes*"; Parvine Mahmoud, "Les Persans de Montesquieu"; also J. L. Carr, "The Secret Chain of the *Lettres persanes.*"

10. *NRF,* I, 1302.

11. *NRF,* I, 1311.

12. *NRF,* I, 1308.

13. But we must not conclude that Montesquieu ever seriously wished to disown the novel. He was understandably concerned with criticisms of the *Letters* in 1728 when such criticism threatened his entrance into the Academy. But as late as 1752 he writes to his friend, Guasco, of Huart's wanting to publish a new edition of the *Letters* and adds only "but there are some *juvenilia* I should like to touch up first." Perhaps he welcomed a new edition of the *Letters* (slightly corrected) as reply to the recent attack of Abbé Gaultier, *Les Lettres persanes convaincues d'impiété* (*The Persian Letters adjudged ungodly*) 1751. *Nagel,* III, 1441 (see also note (d)).

14. Père Desmolets to Montesquieu, 1725. *Nagel,* III, 789.

15. *Nagel,* III, 792.

16. As Villemain so aptly puts it in his *Eloge de Montesquieu:* "Montesquieu gave himself over to the influence of his century, but once he had found a subject worthy of his strength, he became again simple and natural."

17. *NRF,* II, 1374.

18. For details of some aspects of this confusion, see George May, *Le Dilemme du roman au XVIIIe siècle* (New Haven: Yale University Press, 1963); also, critical edition of *Histoire véritable,* edited by Roger Caillois. Spain had already experienced this problem of story-history as evidenced by the insistence on *verdidera* before and after the publication of that "first" novel, the theme of which embroiders on this very problem—*Don Quixote.*

19. "Liberty is achieved only by brilliant strokes, but it is lost by an imperceptible force." *NRF,* II, 211.

20. Montesquieu is certainly and ever conscious of the etymology behind the word he has chosen for his republican principle; there is much *vir-*, manliness and bravery, in the conception as used in the *Romans* and even later at times in *The Spirit,* although in later editions he will make much of having meant by virtue, "political virtue."

21. This early conviction touching upon the influence of Germanic customs on European states will become a long and thorough study of the matter appended to *The Spirit* as Chapters XXX and XXXI.

22. Montesquieu was in the earlier years of his career enamored of the Stoic sect (as it were, the counterpart of the Epicureans) as the following excerpt from his correspondence makes clear: "I admit that their moral code [the Stoics] struck me and that I was quite ready, like M. Dacier, to make a saint of Marcus Aurelius." To Fitz-James, 1750; *Nagel,* III, 1327.

23. Robert Shackleton, *Montesquieu, a Critical Biography.*

24. *L'Esprit des Lois* is most properly translated as *The Spirit of Laws,* although as shown by Montesquieu's correspondence, some contemporary Englishmen preferred *The Genius of Laws.* There is, how-

ever, a slight linguistic problem that, to my knowledge, has never been clarified. The French reads "The Spirit of *the* Laws" and could have expressed "The Spirit of Laws" (in general) by writing *L'Esprit de Lois*. However, in many writers of the century (Diderot, Rousseau, *et. al.*) and elsewhere in Montesquieu (cf. Correspondance, *Nagel*, III, 1199 "On n'a pas des yeux."), the usage would seem to be to use the definite *des* for the more general *de* in similar positions. It is very possible that Montesquieu found his title in a work by Jean Domat (1689): *De la nature et de l'esprit des lois.* See on this, Ernst Klimowsky, *Die englische gewaltenteilungslehre bis zu Montesquieu* (Berlin: Rothschild, 1927).

25. See Charles Vellay, "La genèse de *l'Esprit des Lois.*"

26. "It will be read, appreciated and, bit by bit, adopted by right-thinking people." Jacob Vernet to Montesquieu, 1749. *Nagel*, III, 1257.

27. Montesquieu however insisted that they belonged there and, according to the interpretation of organization one gives to *The Spirit*, he is, no doubt, right. "To make my work complete, I must be able to finish two chapters on feudal laws. I believe I have made discoveries on a matter, the most obscure matter we have, which is nonetheless a magnificent one." (Montesquieu to Mgr. Cerati, 1748, *Nagel*, III, 1116). Vernet, the Protestant scholar who helped him see *The Spirit* through to publication, and offered much helpful critical advice, suggested on this score: "And finally shouldn't you make a part for Roman laws, one expressly for French laws and another for feudal laws? For they are rather distinct. [Vernet is discussing Montesquieu's desire to divide the work in Parts, as well as Books and Chapters.] I confess that the work seems to me to get along well enough with only a Book division. . . ." Vernet to Montesquieu, 1748, *Nagel*, III, 1130. Vernet would seem to understand only partially Montesquieu's intent in including the last two long books (on feudal laws) in *The Spirit*. He adds, however, another suggestion: "Would it be to the point . . . to add (besides the explicative addition to the title we have agreed upon): *with new research on Roman laws touching upon succession, on French laws and on feudal laws.*" This text is exactly what Montesquieu did add to the general title.

28. Typical notes of Montesquieu about his work follow. "As to my *Laws*, I work at it 8 hours a day. The work is immense and I feel I have wasted any time spent on other things. There will be 4 volumes in-12°, 84 books . . . but I shall demand that you say nothing to me about it until you have read it in entirety if you choose to read it, and I dare say that I do not believe the reader will lose his time by the abundance of material." (To Barbot, 1741, *Nagel*, III, 1011.) "As for me, my work progresses as my forces diminish. . . . If I were not

mad, I should not write a line. But what drives me to despair is to see the wonderful things I could do if I had eyes." (To Barbot, 1742, *Nagel,* III, 1015.) "I am overwhelmed with fatigue; I count upon resting the remainder of my days." (To Cerati, 1747, *Nagel,* III, 1083.)

29. This passage forecasts J.-J. Rousseau and his theories of social man's loss of equality in society in the two discourses, and in the *Social Contract*. Rousseau took this loss to be a necessary although unnatural evil; Montesquieu treats it as a fact and studies its consequences for the law. What invites (or can invite) directly to revolution in Rousseau, invites to continual although vigilant adherence to law in Montesquieu.

30. A clear accusation levied against Louis XIV who reduced France's nobility to royal retainers at Versailles. By excess centralization about his person, he deprived the nobility of local (provincial) responsibility and self-respect. Montesquieu would have said he destroyed in them honor, the very principle of monarchy.

31. De Lolme, Montesquieu's interpreter in England, will find his principle of organization—still keeping Montesquieu's separation of powers—in the realization that this idea could (and should) read, "all that the laws do not prohibit."

32. An important qualifier. Montesquieu does not fix his notion of interplay of separate power in adamant form. The separation supposes growth and change of detail.

33. This was one of the chief sources of criticism against *The Spirit* by organized religious (Catholic) opinion.

34. In *Dossier de l'Esprit des Lois*. *NRF*, II, 1029.

35. A representative collection of critical comment from Montesquieu's friends follows from his correspondence. From Jacob Vernet: "Monsieur, what fine lessons you give to the human race, and how well you teach us how we should read history, and how we should travel." (*Nagel,* III, 1118). "There is pleasure in seeing certain maxims of international law make a little progress in the world and your work will spread even more of them from which posterity will gather the fruit." (*Nagel,* III, 1124). From Madame de Tencin: "Here, my dear Roman, is what I think of the *Spirit of Laws*: Philosophy, Reason, Humanity have joined to compose that work and the Graces have taken care to adorn its erudition. . . . I have read it greedily and should be irritated to have finished once and for all a reading experience in which heart, mind and common sense find equal satisfaction." (*Nagel,* III, 1148). From the Chevalier d'Aydie: "I confess as to myself, never having had before any knowledge of these truths so well developed by you, that I am enraptured to learn them, but I imagine that the book will serve its purpose and that in the future it will serve to make wiser kings, ministers and people." (*Nagel,* III, 1159). From

Madame Geoffrin: "This book seems to me the masterpiece of wit, philosophy, metaphysics and wisdom. The choice of subject is a proof of the depth of genius of its author and the manner in which he writes it makes patent the extent of that genius. The book is written with elegance, finesse, precision and nobility." (*Nagel,* III, 1164). From Helvétius: "Our pettifogging legal-eagles are in no shape to read you or to judge you. As to our aristocrats and despots of every sort, if they can understand you, they must not hold too much of a grudge against you. That's the reproach I have always made to your principles." (*Nagel,* III, 1103). From Fontenelle (by way of Chevalier d'Aydie): "Then M. de Fontenelle put in a lively word and held that the book was at once very good and very well written; and afterwards he asked if any bright wit of the world would not be very flattered to have the work attributed to him, supposing the author unknown. I said nobody could be in better position to answer that question than himself: 'As for me,' he replied, throwing out his arms, 'I should adopt it with the greatest joy and be greatly honored to do so.'" (*Nagel,* III, 1233). From his English friend, Charles Yorke: "Since I had the happiness of seeing you, I have read over and over your *Esprit des Loix,* in which I find new things every time I review it, the profoundest knowledge of human nature and government, joined with the greatest elegance of wit, freedom of thought and candour of mind." (In English in original; *Nagel,* III, 1379.) From Président Hénault: "This work, as philosophic as it is scholarly, would be attributed to the finest mind of England if it didn't belong to us by right for its finesse, grace, delicacy and lightness of touch." (*Nagel,* III, 1185.)

36. For some idea of this quaint yet fascinating eccentric, maker of many projects, inventor of a color-organ, see the interminable letters written by Castel to Montesquieu in the correspondence (*Nagel,* III). Montesquieu had known Castel since he had sent his son off to study with Castel's order. The letter of pique, 1748–49 (*Nagel,* III, 1153). Unfortunately, there is no letter of Montesquieu to Castel now existing; one should like to know how the président handled such a verbose correspondent.

37. Placed officially on the *Index,* after long negotiations between the Vatican and Montesquieu's representatives, November 29, 1751. See lengthy correspondence on the matter in *Nagel,* III, 1363 sqq.

38. Except, of course, that this was not Montesquieu's intention. Perhaps Books XXVI and XXIX followed by XXVII might have given a logical conclusion, for Book XXVII (on Roman succession) fits best into Montesquieu's plan of giving an example of his method at work, after the exposition of the spirit of laws—See p. 135. And he speaks of that book as "bringing his work to a close." In actual fact, he did not, of course, bring his work to a close even with that study. For, as his

correspondence makes clear (cf. note 27), when the bulk of his work was already at the printers he considered Book XXVIII (on changes in French law), and Books XXX and XXXI (theory of feudal laws in the establishment and changes in Frankish [European] monarchy), as other necessary "examples" to complete his work.

CHAPTER THREE

1. *NRF*, II, 237. *Esprit des lois,* I, 3. The full quotation continues: "insofar as it governs all the peoples of the earth; and the political and civil laws of each nation must be only particular cases where this human reason is applied." It is an important quotation. One must readily assume that Montesquieu (under the chapter heading of positive law) is here suggesting international law as the most *general* positive law. Yet an equally logical reading is that all law—natural as well as positive—is human reason, since human reason partakes of the prime reason and prime Justice that is God.

2. *NRF*, II, 237.

3. Originally written in 1811, for his American friends, especially Thomas Jefferson. He finally published it to prevent its being further pirated in corrupt form.

4. Robert Shackleton, *Montesquieu,* p. 246.

5. As early as the fragmentary but important *Traité des devoirs* (read before the Bordeaux Academy but never finished because Montesquieu felt his inadequacy to emulate Cicero on the subject), he had written in the *Pensées:* "If men establish societies, it is from a principle of justice. They had it therefore"; and he had insisted in the *Treatise* that justice does not depend on human law. See also *The Persian Letters,* where, even earlier, in Letter #83, Usbek had held that "Justice is a true relationship . . . between two things."

6. *Nagel,* III, 579. Quoted in R. Shackleton, *Montesquieu,* p. 257.

7. There is, naturally, a wide divergence in their views when one considers the source of authority. Hobbes' whole frame of thought depends upon the authority admitted and accepted in the *de facto* chief magistrate (prince or king). That is to say, the positive law really becomes the total explanation of authority and morality. For Montesquieu, authority more and more devolves naturally on the governed (the people), and moral principle (although relative to many determinants as shown so well in *The Persian Letters* and *The Spirit*) must be retraced eventually, beyond state and government, to the absolute of the natural law. That is why Montesquieu (in the Troglodytes and continually thereafter) must disagree with Hobbes' peace-war concept. The very admission of any priority granted to war as a natural law would have vitiated all of Montesquieu's most cherished convictions.

8. *NRF*, I, 1302–3.

9. *NRF*, II, 558 (Book XIX, chapter 4). In the *Pensées* (*NRF*, I, 1458), the list is given as follows: "Men are governed by five different things: climate, manners, customs, Religion and laws. In every nation, as one of these causes operates with more force, the others yield to it by so much. Climate rules almost alone over savages; manners govern the Chinese; laws tyrannize Japan; customs in times past set the tone in Rome and Sparta; and, in our day, Religion is everything in the south of Europe."

10. For example: "Monsieur de St-Aulaire says quite rightly: 'We say: "We cannot understand how matter can think, therefore we have a soul different from matter." Thus we conclude from our ignorance a reason for making ourselves a substance more perfect than matter.'" *NRF*, I, 1540.

11. *Leviathan*, chapter 21.

12. *NRF*, I, 1431.

13. *NRF*, I, 548.

14. *NRF*, I, 539.

15. *NRF*, I, 876. In general, the influence of Montesquieu's travels through republics (Venice, Holland, etc.) upon his political thinking must not be underestimated. A growing predilection for the republican form of government prior to 1728 is conditioned and dampened by his first-hand experience in these countries.

16. *NRF*, I, 880.

17. *NRF*, II, 394. Book XI, chapter 2.

18. *NRF*, I, 1430.

19. Robert Shackleton has already weighed the role of Bolingbroke's influence on Montesquieu in "Montesquieu, Bolingbroke and the Separation of Powers."

20. A first essay was published along with this one in 1690.

21. R. Shackleton, *Montesquieu*, p. 287.

22. See particularly Domville's letter to Montesquieu, June 4, 1749. *Nagel*, III, 1235.

23. Bolingbroke, *The Craftsman*, June 27, 1730; quoted in Shackleton, *Montesquieu*, p. 299; "The first edition of Montesquieu's *Spirit* appeared in 1748, at a time when there was as yet no account of the constitutional law of England which a foreigner could understand. The first edition of Blackstone's *Commentaries* appears in 1765, and proceeded in many respects on the fundamental results reached by Montesquieu. The subsequent editions of those two celebrated works went henceforth side by side as the chief sources from which politicians took their view of constitutionalism. The sources from which Montesquieu drew were, unmistakably, the party pamphlets of the Whigs and Tories under George II, in which, from love to the Revolution of 1688, the original legal bases of the constitution were already, with the silent

consent too of both parties, entirely displaced. The French commentators on Montesquieu went no farther back at the utmost than to certain citations from Blackstone, without in any way troubling themselves to try to comprehend the legal coherence and connection of the English political system." *Der Rechtsstaat,* p. 189. Quoted in Robert Flint, *Philosophy of History in Europe,* p. 102.

24. See chapter 1, note 3 above.

25. Read particularly Book XXIV, chapters 2 and 6 of *The Spirit.* Also in the *Defense of the Spirit,* second objection.

26. "I should not wish for missionaries to go preach to the Chinese; for, since they would have to point out to the Chinese the falsity of their religion, the Chinese would become bad citizens before they could be made into Christians." *NRF,* I, 1322.

27. "For, after all, the history of a Christian nation ought to be the practical morality of Christianity." *NRF,* I, 1380.

28. "What proves to me the necessity of [religious] revelation, is the inadequacy of natural Religion, or the fear or superstition of man." *NRF,* I, 1550.

29. "When it is said that there is no absolute quality, it doesn't mean that there is none at all, but that there is none in us and that our mind cannot resolve such qualities." *NRF,* I, 1537.

30. *NRF,* II, 387 (*Spirit,* Book X, chapter 13). Robert Flint (*Philosophy of History,* p. 105) discerns quite rightly, it seems to me, a major contribution of Montesquieu in this distinction between accidental and inherent: "In this book there is an enunciation, proof, and varied application of the great principle which Montesquieu had already exemplified in so masterly a manner in the *Grandeur* (*Romans*): the epoch-making principle that the course of history is on the whole determined by general causes, by widespread and persistent tendencies, by broad and deep undercurrents, and only influenced in a feeble, secondary and subordinate degree by single events, by definite arguments, by particular enactments, by anything accidental, isolated or individual."

31. He wrote, however, the following provocative comment: "I said: 'The Catholic Religion will destroy the protestant Religion and then, Catholics will become Protestants.'" *NRF,* I, 1567.

32. *NRF,* I, 1152.

33. *NRF,* I, 982; *NRF,* I, 1153.

34. *NRF,* I, 1481–84.

35. *NRF,* I, 1537.

36. *Nagel,* III, 1235.

37. *NRF,* I, 1058.

38. *NRF,* I, 1460.

39. *NRF,* I, 393.

40. Bolingbroke, *The Craftsman,* June 27, 1730, quoted in Robert Shackleton, *Montesquieu,* p. 165.

41. *NRF,* I, 1434.

42. *NRF,* I, 1458.

43. *NRF,* I, 1541. Strong, in the original: ". . . que toute la philosophie consiste dans ces trois mots: Je m'en f. . . ."

44. *NRF,* I, 981.

CHAPTER FOUR

1. "I ask nothing more of the earth save that it continue to turn on its center." *Nagel,* III, 1072.

2. Helvétius retired from his lucrative post of farmer of taxes in 1751 to devote himself to ideas.

3. *Nagel,* III, 1102.

4. *Nagel,* III, 1103.

5. *Nagel,* III, 1539.

6. In A. L. C. Destutt de Tracy, *Commentaires sur l'Esprit des lois* (Paris: Desoer, 1819; also in same title, in English, [Philadelphia: Duane, 1811]).

7. *Ibid.*

8. Voltaire spoke of Montesquieu in other places, notably in his *Ecrivains français du siècle de Louis XIV* (*Moland,* vol. 14), and in "Remerciment sincère à un homme charitable" (*Moland,* vol. 23) addressed, ironically, to Montesquieu's critic in the *Nouvelles ecclésiastiques* (April 24, 1750), attacking Montesquieu's *Defense of the Spirit.*

9. See D. C. Cabeen: "The *esprit* of the *Esprit des lois*" in *PMLA,* 1939. For Montesquieu's succinct rejoinder, see *Nagel,* III, 1435.

10. In Philadelphia, published by Duane. See note 6, above.

CHAPTER FIVE

1. Quoted in Fletcher, *Montesquieu and English Politics,* p. 21.

2. See particularly F. T. H. Fletcher, *Montesquieu and English Politics (1750–1800)*. Also, R. S. Crane, "Montesquieu and British Thought." For Swift, see H. Jannsen, *Montesquieu's Theorie von der Dreistellung der Gewalten im Staate auf ihre Quellen zurück geführt* (Gotha, 1878).

3. Quoted in Fletcher, *op. cit.,* p. 33.

4. Gibbon in *Mixed Writings,* I, 96 (quoted in Fletcher, *op. cit.*) says: "Locke's *Treatise of Government* instructed me in the knowledge of Whig principles: . . . but my delight was in the frequent perusal of Montesquieu whose energy of style and boldness of hypothesis were powerful to awaken and stimulate the genius of the age."

5. Of this Montesquieu was aware, as shown in his letter to Hume

in 1749. "I prefer to speak to you of a fine dissertation in which you give to moral causes a much greater influence than to physical causes; and it seemed to me (insofar as I can judge) that the subject is treated thoroughly, however difficult it be, and written by the hand of a master, and filled with very new ideas and reflections." *Nagel,* III, 1230.

6. Fletcher, *op. cit.,* p. 119 sqq.

7. Barbot adds: "When shall we see this good book quoted in the council of the King of France?" Barbot to Montesquieu, 1749. *Nagel,* III, 1216.

8. *Nagel,* III, 1239. Montesquieu was not without having some playful jibes made at him in explanation of his Anglophilism. Solar de Brille writes to him pointedly: "You are the friend of the English who buy your wines." *Nagel,* III, 1242.

9. *Nagel,* III, 1235. It is in this letter that Domville shows he has understood Montesquieu's indirect warning to the British. "You feel that we are no longer what we ought to be, that our liberty has turned to license, that the very idea of the common weal is lost and that the fate of rich and corrupt nations awaits us—even that we are hurrying toward it headlong."

10. Fletcher, *op. cit.,* p. 174.

11. *Ibid.,* p. 141.

12. Blackstone, *Commentaries,* I, 269 (quoted in Fletcher, p. 138).

13. Paul Janet, *Histoire de la science politique dans ses rapports avec la morale,* II, 400–1.

14. Thomas Regnault, *Tableaux analytiques de Montesquieu suivis de la comparaison de plusieurs principaux passages de Montesquieu et de Blackstone* (Paris, 1824).

15. Edmund Burke, quoted in Fletcher, *op. cit.,* p. 132.

16. Edmund Burke, quoted in Fletcher, *op. cit.,* p. 243. "After 1789 the direct influence of Montesquieu in England is slight, but he was in Burke's eyes a model of all that was greatest in the *ancien régime* discredited at the time of the Revolution. In France, Montesquieu was being attacked because he had defended the French and British constitutions. It is Burke who, in a sense, defends Montesquieu and continues the tradition for which the great French thinker stands." C. P. Courtney, *Montesquieu and Burke,* p. 184. How close Burke comes to the truth might be suggested by Mirabeau's reaction to the mention of the name of Montesquieu: "The outdated reveries of that man are no longer respected except in some northern courts."

17. Philarète Chasles, *Le XVIIIe siècle en Angleterre,* p. 213 (quoted in Fletcher, *op. cit.,* p. 250–1).

18. See Fletcher, *op. cit.,* p. 254.

19. Jeremy Bentham, *Works,* X, 54 (Bouring edition).

20. *Ibid.,* I, 162.

21. Cesare de Beccaria, *Dei delitti e delle pene*, 1764. Beccaria in that work expresses his debt to Montesquieu. "L'immortale Presidente Montesquieu ha rapidamente scorso su di questa materia. L'indivisible Verità mi ha sforzato a seguire le tracce di questo Grand'Uomo; ma gli uomini pensatori, per li quale scrivo, sapranno distinguere i miei passi da' suoi." pp. 5–6. ("The immortal Président Montesquieu rapidly mastered this material. Indivisible Truth has forced me to follow in the steps of that Great Man; but men who think, those for whom I write, will know how to distinguish my steps from his.")

22. Paul Spurlin, *Montesquieu in America.* Also, Hermann Knust, *Der Staatsaufklärer Montesquieu.* The article by Sergio Cotta (see Bibliography) is the best summation of the whole problem.

23. Consult Gilbert Chinard, *Pensées choisies de Montesquieu tirées du Commonplace Book de Thomas Jefferson.*

24. John Adams, *Works,* VI, 205–6 (quoted in Spurlin, p. 190).

25. Spurlin, *op. cit.*, p. 220.

26. James Madison, in the Virginia Convention debates on the Constitution, quoted in Spurlin, p. 261.

CHAPTER SIX

1. It was Fustel de Coulanges (1830–89) who attacked, toward the end of his career, the general theory of Germanic influence on feudalism to which Montesquieu had devoted so many pages in *The Spirit.*

CHAPTER SEVEN

1. Fletcher, "The Poetics of *l'Esprit* . . . ," p. 317.

2. *NRF*, I, 1428.

3. Benjamin Cardozo, *The Growth of Law,* p. 52 (quoted in Huntington Cairns, *Law and the Social Sciences,* p. 13).

4. Bronislaw Malinowski, *Crime and Custom in Savage Society,* p. 9 (quoted in Cairns, *op. cit.*, p. 16).

5. Paul Janet, *Histoire de la science politique,* II, 400–401.

6. Montesquieu to Solar, 1749. *Nagel,* III, 1200.

7. Cairns, *op. cit.*, p. 28.

8. *Ibid.*, p. 59.

9. Not all certainly. A recent work on Montesquieu by a sociologist is filled with valuable and sympathetic insight into his contributions to the social sciences—W. Stark, *Montesquieu Pioneer of the Sociology of Knowledge* (London: Routledge, 1960). Charles E. Vaughan (in *Studies in the History of Political Philosophy* . . . , p. 255) points out that Montesquieu's soul contained "two men struggling for the mastery: the political philosopher and the practical reformer." Millar, the nineteenth-century social scientist, said that: "The great Montesquieu pointed out the road. He was the Lord Bacon in this branch of science.

Dr. Smith is the Newton." Trevor-Roper, the eminent contemporary British historian, speaking of the "explosive decade" of the 1740's, remarks: "All the same it seems odd that the greatest outcry was caused by that innocent, majestic work of scholarship, the foundation of modern sociology, published in Geneva in 1748: Montesquieu's *L'Esprit des lois*" (*The New Statesman,* October 17, 1961).

10. Flint, *Philosophy of History,* p. 96.

11. *NRF,* I, 1286.

12. *NRF,* I, 1537.

13. Probably for this very reason, Montesquieu has been frequently criticized for having made no distinction between government and State, and for having drawn no clear and generally valid definition of the State. This criticism is particularly pointed in Otto Gierke's work, *Natural Law and the Theory of Society.* "In dealing with the theory of separation of powers," says Gierke, "Montesquieu avoids entirely any treatment of the problem of sovereignty. . . . He never makes any reference whatever to the personality of the State." Or again: ". . . Montesquieu fails to draw any practical conclusions from his recognition of the basic rights of the community . . . so far from doing so, he entirely omits the conception of the unity of sovereignty (just as he omits the conception of the State as a whole) from the picture he draws of the constitutional state." Gierke shows most clearly his divergence from Montesquieu in his succinct comment upon what these last pages have attempted to show as Montesquieu's great virtue, when he says: "Montesquieu never transcends the idea of society as the product of intelligent individuals." Gierke, *op. cit.,* (Boston: Beacon Press, 1960), pp. 352, 153, 104.

14. *NRF,* I, 1465, 1464, 1226, 1284; II, 1278, 1403, 1412.

15. See chapter 1, note 19.

16. Montesquieu to Hénault. *Nagel,* III, 1186.

17. *NRF,* I, 671.

Selected Bibliography

PRIMARY SOURCES

The Persian Letters. Trans., ed., introd., by J. Robert Loy. New York: World (Meridian), 1961.

Considerations on the Causes of the Greatness of the Romans and their Decline. Trans. David Lowenthal. New York: Free Press, 1965.

The Spirit of Laws. New York: Hafner, 1949.

Oeuvres complètes (publiées sous la direction d'André Masson). Paris: Nagel, 1950–55. 3 vols.

Oeuvres complètes (ed. Roger Caillois). Paris, Gallimard (Pléiade), 1951. 2 vols.

Les Lettres persanes. Ed. Paul Vernière. Paris: Garnier, 1960.

Les Lettres persanes (ed. critique par Antoine Adam). Geneva: Droz, 1954.

De l'esprit des lois (ed. Jean Brèthe de la Gressaye). Paris: Les Belles Lettres, 1950–58.

Histoire véritable (ed. critique par Roger Caillois). Geneva: Droz, 1948.

SECONDARY SOURCES

CABEEN, DAVID C. *Montesquieu: a Bibliography.* New York: New York Public Library Bulletin, June-October, 1947.

———. "A Supplementary Montesquieu Bibliography," *Revue internationale de philosophie*, XXXIII–XXXIV (1951).

——— (ed). *A Critical Bibliography of French Literature (18th Century).* Syracuse: Syracuse University Press, 1951 (*Supplement*, Ed. Rich. Brooks, 1968). Montesquieu compiled by Cabeen and Loy.

BERLIN, ISAIAH. "Montesquieu," read October 19, 1955; *Pub. Brit. Acad.*, XLI (1955), 267–96.

BONNO, GABRIEL. "Montesquieu's *Esprit des lois* and its Significance for the Modern World," *French-American Review*, II (1949), 1–11. Good reappraisal of Montesquieu's role after 200 years.

CAIRNS, HUNTINGTON. *Law and the Social Sciences.* New York: Harcourt, Brace, 1935. Excellent chapter on Montesquieu's role in theory of separation of powers.

COTTA, SERGIO. "Montesquieu, la séparation des pouvoirs et la constitution fédérale des Etats-Unis," *Revue d'histoire politique et constitutionelle,* IV (1951), 225–47. Best recent estimate of Montesquieu's role among Founding Fathers, weighing all past thinking on subject.

COURTNEY, C. P. *Montesquieu and Burke.* Oxford: Blackwell, 1963. Well-documented survey of career of Burke with comment on probable influence by Montesquieu on Burke's thinking during various periods of English history at close of 18th century.

CRISAFULLI, A. S. "Parallels to ideas in the *Lettres persanes,*" *PMLA,* LII (1937), 773–77. Important study showing moral and social ideas which Montesquieu had in common with Malebranche, Leibnitz, and Shaftesbury.

DURKHEIM, EMILE. *Montesquieu and Rousseau.* Preface by Henri Peyre. Ann Arbor, Mich.: University of Michigan Press, 1960. Seminal article by France's father of sociology on Montesquieu's contribution to political science.

EHRARD, JEAN. *Montesquieu, Critique D'art.* (Publ. Faculté des Lettres et Sciences Humaines de l'Université de Clermont-Ferrand). Paris, Presses Univ., 1965.

FLETCHER, F. T. H. *Montesquieu and English Politics (1750–1800).* London: Arnold, 1939. Important study comparing Montesquieu to Adam Smith, Blackstone, Locke, Hume, and Gibbon.

GRIMSLEY, RONALD. "The Idea of Nature in the *Lettres persanes,*" *French Studies* V (1951), 293–306. Serious article proposing to study norms of *reason* and *nature* as used by Montesquieu in *Persian Letters.*

LEVIN, LAWRENCE M. *The Political Doctrine of Montesquieu's "Esprit des lois": its Classical Background.* New York: Institute of French Studies, 1936. Essential work, well-documented.

OAKE, ROGER. "Montesquieu's Religious Ideas," *Journal of the History of Ideas,* XIV (1953), 548–60. Perceptive article distinguishing between Montesquieu's traditional Catholicism and his intellectual inquiry.

———. "Montesquieu's Analysis of Roman History," *Journal of the History of Ideas* XVI (1955), 44–59. Important article showing that Rome's success, for Montesquieu, was neither a proof of divine plan nor an ideal model for politicians.

PAPPAS, JOHN. *Berthier's Journal de Trévoux and the Philosophes* (Chapter on Montesquieu). (*Studies on Voltaire and the Eighteenth Century,* Vol. 3). Geneva, Institut et Musée Voltaire, 1957.

SHACKLETON, ROBERT. *Montesquieu, a Critical Biography.* London: Oxford, 1961. Essential study of man and works. Most complete and careful treatment in English by eminent scholar.

SPURLIN, PAUL M. *Montesquieu in America, 1760–1801.* University, La.: Louisiana State University Press, 1940. Essential study become classic. Careful preparation of basis for estimating Montesquieu's influence on American colonies.

STAROBINSKI, JEAN. *Montesquieu par lui-même.* Paris: Ed. du Seuil, 1961. Excellent, short Man and Works in French. Provocative, long introduction, excellent choice of representative texts from *Works* (in French) and interesting iconography, etc.

VAUGHAN, CHARLES E. *Studies in the History of Political Philosophy before and after Rousseau.* New York: Longmans, Green, 1925. Important study of Montesquieu (along with Vico) in chapter entitled "The Eclipse of Contract."

Note: To avoid repetition, pertinent information about all studies not fully listed in Notes and Bibliography is to be found in *A Critical Bibliography of French Literature,* listed above. Carr (note #9, Chapter II) as well as other provocative articles on Montesquieu and the eighteenth century are to be found in *Proceedings, Second International Congress on the Enlightenment,* to be published 1967 or 1968. Particularly, Paul H. Meyer, "Politics and Morals in the Thought of Montesquieu."

Index